S. BARNES

ASSIGN [Filename] SYS$OUTPUT
[DEBUG

DE ASSIGN   SYS$OUTPUT

Assembly Language Programming for the VAX-11

Little, Brown Computer Systems Series

Gerald M. Weinberg, Editor

Barnett, Michael P., and Graham K. Barnett
Personal Graphics for Profit and Pleasure on the Apple II Plus Computer

Basso, David T., and Ronald D. Schwartz
Programming with FORTRAN/WATFOR/WATFIV

Chattergy, Rahul, and Udo W. Pooch
Top-down, Modular Programming in FORTRAN with WATFIV

Coats, R. B., and A. Parkin
Computer Models in the Social Sciences

Conway, Richard, and David Gries
An Introduction to Programming: A Structured Approach Using PL/I and PL/C, Third Edition

Conway, Richard, and David Gries
Primer on Structured Programming: Using PL/I, PL/C, and PL/CT

Conway, Richard, David Gries, and E. Carl Zimmerman
A Primer on Pascal, Second Edition

Cripps, Martin
An Introduction to Computer Hardware

Easley, Grady M.
Primer for Small Systems Management

Finkenaur, Robert G.
COBOL for Students: A Programming Primer

Freedman, Daniel P., and Gerald M. Weinberg
Handbook of Walkthroughs, Inspections, and Technical Reviews: Evaluating Programs, Projects, and Products, Third Edition

Graybeal, Wayne, and Udo W. Pooch
Simulation: Principles and Methods

Greenfield, S. E.
The Architecture of Microcomputers

Greenwood, Frank
Profitable Small Business Computing

Healy, Martin, and David Hebditch
The Microcomputer in On-Line Systems: Small Computers in Terminal-Based Systems and Distributed Processing Networks

Lemone, Karen A., and Martin E. Kaliski
Assembly Language Programming for the VAX-11

Lias, Edward J.
Future Mind: The Microcomputer—New Medium, New Mental Environment

Lines, M. Vardell, and Boeing Computer Services Company
Minicomputer Systems

Mashaw, B. J.
Programming Byte by Byte: Structured FORTRAN 77

Mills, Harlan D.
Software Productivity

Assembly Language Programming for the VAX-11

Karen A. Lemone

Worcester Polytechnic Institute

Martin E. Kaliski

Northeastern University

Little, Brown and Company

Boston   Toronto

Library of Congress Cataloging in Publication Data

Lemone, Karen A.
  Assembly language programming for the VAX-11.

  (Little, Brown computer systems series)
  1. VAX-11 (Computer)—Programming. 2. Assembler
language (Computer program language) I. Kaliski,
Martin E. II. Title. III. Series.
QA76.8.V37L45 1983   001.64'2   82.-22919
ISBN 0-316-52072-1

Library of Congress Catalog Card Number 82-22919

ISBN 0-316-52072-1

9 8 7 6 5 4 3 2 1

MV

Published simultaneously in Canada
by Little, Brown & Company (Canada) Limited

Printed in the United States of America

Disclaimer of Liabilities: Due care has been exercised in the preparation of this book to insure its
effectiveness. The authors and publisher make no warranty, expressed or implied, with respect to
the programs or other contents of this book. In no event will the authors or publishers be liable
for direct, indirect, incidental, or consequential damages in connection with or arising from the
furnishing, performance or use of this book.

To our respective children:
Aliza, Jamie, Jill, Rafael, and ? .

Foreword

Sometimes I worry that my position as Series Editor gives me too much power to indulge my prejudices. For instance, it's very easy for me to reject a book on teaching your turkey to program in FORTRAN, because I'm slightly prejudiced against turkeys, substantially prejudiced against FORTRAN, and completely prejudiced against teaching turkeys to program.

On the other hand, it was very easy for me to accept *Assembly Language Programming for the VAX-11*—and not just because it isn't about FORTRAN or turkeys. Lemone and Kaliski have written a superbly crafted course in assembly language for readers with some prior experience in programming higher level languages. Their effort thus appeals simultaneously to three of my long-standing predilections—for good writing, for assembly language, and for teaching assembly language to anyone seriously interested in the practice of programming. Perhaps I'd better explain my bias in favor of this book, so you can judge for yourself.

It may be difficult to explain my prejudice in favor of good writing because, in the more technical subjects, good writing is so rare that some readers may never have seen it. In reading about a subject like assembly language, many readers get turned off because the writing is poor, not because the subject is difficult. They are novices, and they have no way to separate the dancer from the dance. They simply put down the book and give up on the subject.

But teachers who adopt Lemone and Kaliski's *Assembly Language Programming for the VAX-11* don't have to fear that the writing is going to turn the students against the course. The book is written clearly, with precision, and at just the right level. It is comprehensive without being superficial, detailed without being trivial, and altogether pleasant to read.

How can a book on assembly language be "pleasant to read"? That's my prejudice again! Assembly language was my first language, and my second and third. The first book I ever wrote was on assembly language, as was the first computer course I ever taught. These experiences do give me a bias in favor of assembly language that some may not share, but on the other hand they also give me a prejudice *against* any author who mistreats assembly language. I find Lemone and Kaliski to be sensitive to both the opportunities and limitations of assembly language. If this is prejudice, then I plead guilty.

Assembly language is not just fun to read about—it is an essential part of the education of any true computer professional. The first assembly language course is a pivotal course for the budding computer scientist or electrical engineer. In fact, assembly language is pivotal precisely because it is the meeting ground between the two disciplines. Not every teacher may agree with this prejudice of mine, but after more than a quarter century of training both computer scientists and engineers, I'm not going to be talked out of it easily. I've seen too many students pulling it all together for the first time in the assembly language course.

And pulling it all together is what Lemone and Kaliski do. I particularly like their treatment of assembler design issues as a way of making the course into something more than an unordered collection of random facts. The student who works through *Assembly Language Programming for the VAX-11* will have a real feeling of accomplishing something worthwhile, and will be well prepared to move in any one of several different directions for more depth—hardware design, design of languages, design and implementation of translators, or specific assembly languages on other machines.

So if you are teaching or learning assembly language on the VAX-11, I recommend that you use Lemone and Kaliski's book. But since I am prejudiced, why don't you see for yourself?

Gerald M. Weinberg

Preface

This is a two-part text about assembly language programming in the VAX/ MACRO language. Unlike many texts on assembly language that are concerned solely with the assembly language per se, this text also addresses the design of assemblers, macroprocessors, and linkers. It is divided into two stylistically different parts.

In Part I the fundamentals of assembly language programming in the VAX/ MACRO language are discussed. It is aimed at the beginning assembly language programmer, conforming with current ACM recommendations concerning introductory assembly language programming courses.

Chapter 1 introduces the basic vocabulary and concepts of assembly language programming. It is a learn by doing chapter that encourages the reader to think in assembly language terms and serves to motivate the ensuing discussion in Chapters 2 and 3. In Chapter 2 the VAX organization and architecture are discussed. Chapter 3 covers the binary, decimal, and hexadecimal number systems and describes the ways that data can be stored in memory. Data storage directives are introduced in this chapter.

Chapter 4 describes the various addressing modes in VAX/MACRO and their uses. The instruction set is also introduced. After having completed Chapter 4, the student should be able to write simple programs in the VAX/MACRO language.

Chapter 5 describes some fundamental assembly language programming constructs, relating them to analogous higher-level language constructs (in FORTRAN, BASIC, Pascal, and pseudo-code). Topics such as assignment statements, conditional statements, loops, and array operations are addressed. Chapter 5 is the heart of Part I.

Chapters 6 and 7 discuss, respectively, macros and subroutines/procedures. The reasons for using these techniques are examined, and through the examples of these chapters the material of Chapters 4 and 5 is solidified. Input/output programming is studied in Chapter 8. Because this chapter is highly dependent upon the VAX/VMS operating system, the reader may prefer alternative material on input/output widely available. Chapter 9 provides an introduction to more advanced techniques in assembly language programming, such as conditional assembly and character string manipulation.

The flavor of the discussion changes in Part II of the text: Part II's system viewpoint complements the user's point of view.

Chapter 10 is concerned with the basic issues of assembler design, taking a modular approach to the software design of assemblers. Chapter 11 extends the methodology of Chapter 10 to macroprocessor design issues, and Chapter 12 discusses linker design.

The treatment of these topics in Part II contrasts with the basic approach of Part I. The discussion is more general and the exercises more advanced. It is hoped that this will serve to round out the reader's knowledge of assembly language and assembly language programming techniques.

There are five appendices to this text. Appendix A presents introductory material allowing the reader to use the VAX/VMS operating system. Appendix B highlights the design issues not covered in Chapter 10, as does Appendix D for Chapter 11. Appendices C and E attempt to define a restricted version of VAX/MACRO, called SUBMAC, suitable for use in system software design projects.

Acknowledgments

Although we have made every effort to eliminate errors, it is possible that some still exist. If so, we would appreciate knowing about them. Feel free to write to either of us or to the editors at Little, Brown. If possible, we will answer.

We would like to mention that the errors you *don't* see were detected in previous drafts by the following people (to mention just a few): Brian Alves, Susan Blyde, Willy Burgess, John Crosby, Sharon Giggey, Chris Hacket, Whitney Harris, Ellen Hollis, Lenny Leffand, Riad Loutfi, Steve Morth, Heyedeh Motallabi, Duane Pawson, Hank Thoelke, Richard Tyson, Professor Tom Westervelt, Mark Woodbury, and the entire Winter '81 6.130 class at Northeastern University. We apologize to anyone we have left out! The errors that remain are all ours.

In addition, we would like to thank Professor Richard Carter for having the courage to use this text in some of its previous versions and the people at Massachusetts Computer Associates for sharing their expertise in computering.

This text was typed and edited on line by Laurie Reynolds, Jonathan Chappell, Kathi Marks, Hank Thoelke, Audrey Aduama, and the authors. The excellent drawings are by George Capalbo. Special thanks go to Hank Thoelke for his unselfish help throughout this project.

Karen A. Lemone and Martin E. Kaliski

Contents

Part I

VAX/MACRO Assembly Language

Chapter 1

Getting Started

This chapter introduces the VAX-11 computer and some vocabulary and concepts of assembly language programming.

Readers familiar with a compiler language such as BASIC, COBOL, FORTRAN, or Pascal are familiar with the way a set of instructions solves a problem. These compiler languages deal with inputs and outputs and the algebraic manipulations necessary to convert one (inputs) into the other (outputs). Compiler languages operate on inputs and outputs; there is little need to know what the computer is actually doing with the data. Languages such as assembly language and machine language, however, operate more directly on the machine or the machine parts. For example, arithmetic generally takes place in high-speed storage locations called *registers*. In an assembly language or machine language program, we refer to these registers directly. Thus, we need to know something about registers—how many there are, which ones to use, how to refer to them, what size they are, and so on. Most compiler languages make no mention of registers at all. The compiler decides what registers, if any, to use. But any discussion of assembly language or machine language must include an explanation of registers and various other parts of the computer (known collectively as the machine *architecture*). The VAX machine architecture will be described in Chapter 2. This chapter defines the terms *machine language* and *assembly language* and compares them with *compiler languages*.

1.1 Machine Language and Assembly Language

Machine language

Machine language is the computer's "native" language. There are only two symbols in machine language. These are 0 and 1, which are called binary digits or *bits* for short (from *b*inary dig*it*). Each statement in machine language consists of a sequence of bits called a *bit pattern:*

01010110000000101011010000

An executable computer program is nothing more than a stored collection of bit patterns. These bit patterns are stored in the part of the computer known as *memory*. Each of these bit patterns may represent an instruction, a piece of data, or even the location of an instruction or piece of data.

In the preceding example, the rightmost eight bits represent the instruction called "Move." The next eight bits represent the datum "2," and the leftmost eight bits stand for "Register 6" (denoted by R6):

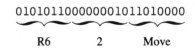

R6   2   Move

Thus the bit pattern for the statement "Move the constant 2 into Register 6" contains an instruction (Move), a piece of data (2), and a reference to a machine part (R6). Notice that the instruction must be read from right to left!

A separate component of the computer called the *central processing unit* (denoted CPU) interprets these bit patterns that have been stored in the computer's memory. The CPU is designed to recognize what is an instruction and what is a datum. It is the CPU that executes a machine language program that has been stored in memory. That is, the CPU understands this machine language. Humans, however, find such sequences of 0's and 1's somewhat incomprehensible and quite difficult to remember. Dealing with bit patterns requires the programmer to remember the numeric code for each instruction and the location in memory of each data item—all in binary. For these reasons we do not write programs in machine language if we can avoid it. Instead we write programs in a more understandable form: *assembly language*.

Assembly language

In assembly language, as in compiler languages, a data item may be addressed by a symbolic name such as *a, min, result, and factorial*. Also a descriptive, mnemonic instruction is used instead of a numeric code.

EXAMPLE

```
movl #2,r6
```

is the VAX-11 assembly language code for the machine code of the previous example. It is much easier to believe and remember that this means "Move a 2 into Register 6."

Unfortunately, computers cannot understand assembly language; they understand only the bit patterns of machine language. Thus, before an assembly language program can be executed, it first must be translated into machine language. A program called an *assembler* performs this translation. (Part II of the text discusses the design of assemblers in greater detail.)

Assembly
language   →   Assembler   →   Machine
program   language
                                      program

EXAMPLE

movl #2,r6 →   VAX-11   →   010101100000001011010000
        .   assembler   .
        .   .
        .   .

There is exactly one machine language instruction for every assembly language instruction.

Compiler language

In languages such as FORTRAN, BASIC, COBOL, and Pascal a program called a compiler frequently translates the instruction into machine language. Consider the FORTRAN statement *a=2* and the Pascal statement *a:=2*.

a=2   →   FORTRAN   →   Sequence of 0's and 1's
            compiler

a:=2   →   Pascal   →   Sequence of 0's and 1's
            compiler

1.2   Thinking in Assembly Language

Calculating 2*3+4

Programming in assembly language is similar to operating a calculator. Each data value must be entered and, in general, each operation such as addition or multiplication must be performed separately. Compiler languages, on the other hand, can frequently perform more than one operation in a single statement. Consider the following assignment statement:

```
result=2*3+4
```

which multiplies 2 times 3, adds 4, and assigns the result to the variable named *result*. (In some languages such as Pascal this would be written "result:=2∗3+4".) To accomplish this statement in assembly language, we must first enter the value 2. Register 6 will be chosen (at random) to hold this value. To enter the number 2 into Register 6:

```
movl #2,r6
```

The instruction *movl* tells the CPU to copy the number 2 into Register 6. Next, multiply the contents of Register 6 by 3:

```
mull2 #3,r6
```

and lastly,

```
addl3 #4,r6,result
```

adds a 4 to the contents of Register 6 and moves a copy of the sum to the *location* whose *symbolic name* is *result*. The entire sequence is

```
movl  #2,r6
mull2 #3,r6
addl3 #4,r6,result
```

and is one way of calculating 2∗3+4 and storing the answer at the location whose name is *result*.

Instruction parts

Notice that there are two parts to each of the instructions above—an operation and some operands (we will see two optional parts later):

```
movl    #2,r6
  ↑       ↑
Operation Operands
```

Some operations end in 2 (e.g., *mull2*). This indicates that there are two operands (e.g., #2 and R6). Similarly, an instruction ending in 3 has three operands. For example, *addl3* above has three parts to its operand—#4, R6, and *result*. Note that some instructions (e.g., *movl*) have neither a 2 nor a 3, which indicates a fixed number of operands. *movl* always has two operands.

Calculating a∗b+c

Next, consider the more general case of calculating a∗b+c and storing the answer in *result:*

```
result=a∗b+c
```

In VAX assembly language this becomes

```
movl     a,r6
mull2    b,r6
addl3    c,r6,result
```

In the last instruction, the contents of the memory location denoted by *c* are added to the contents of Register 6 and the sum is stored in the location whose symbolic name is *result*.

Reserving memory

In order to calculate the assignment statement

```
result:=a*b+c
```

values must be assigned to the variables *a*, *b*, and *c*. In our VAX assembly language program

```
movl     a,r6
mull2    b,r6
addl3    c,r6,result
```

a, *b*, *c*, and *result* are symbolic names for memory locations. Thus, a memory location must be reserved for each of them. In addition, *a*, *b*, and *c* must be assigned values. (The value for *result* is calculated by the program.) The instruction

```
a:  .long 2
```

allots 32 bits of memory (called a *longword*) and puts a 2 into it. (We did not need anywhere near this much space to store a 2!) Similarly,

```
b:  .long 3   and   c:  .long 4
```

put aside 32 bits each for *b* and *c* and initialize them to 3 and 4, respectively. The instruction

```
result:  .long
```

puts aside 32 bits for the symbolic name *result*. Note that no initial value is assigned to this location. When no initial value is assigned to a longword, the memory location is assigned the value 0.

The complete program

There are the usual instructions denoting the beginning and end of the program. The instructions

```
start:    .word
              .
              .
              .
        .end start
```

tell the assembler where the beginning and end of the executable program are. *start* is not a magic word here. Any other symbolic name may be used. The operand for *.end* (*start* here) tells the assembler the symbolic name of the first executable instruction of the program. The assembler does not translate any instructions occurring after the *.end* instruction.

> *Symbolic names* may be up to 31 characters in length. They can consist of letters, digits, underlines (_), dollar signs ($), and periods (.). The first character must not be a digit.

The instruction

```
ret
```

terminates execution of the program. The entire program is shown in Figure 1-1.

Capitalization

The reader may have noticed that we have not been writing our programs in capital letters. We prefer to code in small letters. Many people prefer to code their programs in capitals. It really doesn't matter. The VAX/VMS assembler allows you to use *result, RESULT,* and *Result.* They are all the same symbolic name.

Symbolic addresses

It is important to distinguish between a location and the contents at that location. Consider, for example, the memory location referred to by the first line of Figure 1-1. The symbolic name for that location (sometimes called a symbolic *address*) is *a*. During execution, this symbolic address corresponds to some actual (unknown-to-us) location in memory. The contents of the location whose name is *a* is 2 (actually 0. . .010). To repeat: there is some location in memory; *a* is the name of that location and 2 is the contents at that location. In this text we will call *a*

Symbolic Address

Figure 1–1.

```
a:        .long    2
b:        .long    3
c:        .long    4
result:  .long
start:    .word
          movl     a,r6
          mull2    b,r6
          addl3    c,r6,result
last:     ret
          .end     start
```

the symbolic address or just address. In addition, we will frequently say "location *a*" as a shorthand for the "location whose name is *a*."

Assembling

The assembler changes these instructions into machine language so that they may be loaded (in the next step) into the computer's memory.

Each operation such as *movl* must be translated into its own unique bit pattern called an opcode (operation code). This opcode (11010000 for *movl*) is built into the computer's circuitry.

Loading

The set of instructions is stored sequentially in memory. The loader (or linker) assigns these sequential addresses to the program. Linkers are discussed in Part II in greater detail.

Executing

The address where the first instruction is stored is automatically put into a register when the program begins execution. When the CPU has finished executing the first instruction, it updates this register to contain the address of the next instruction. The CPU does this by adding the amount of memory space occupied by the previous instruction to the previous contents of the register. Since this register is thus "counting" through the program, it is called the program counter (denoted PC).

1.3   A More Complicated Example

The program in Section 1.2 (Figure 1-1) is an example of a "straight-line" program. It contains no loops or decision (conditional) statements. In this section we will look at a program which contains a loop.

Pseudo-Code

The following algorithm (set of instructions) calculates 10-factorial (10!). It could be coded easily into any compiler language:

```
fact:=1
loop for i:=1 to 10
          fact:=fact*i
end   loop
```

These four lines are pseudo-code for calculating 10-factorial. Pseudo-code is used when we wish to describe the steps needed to solve a problem more formally than we can in English but not so formally that we wish to use a particular language. The first line initializes *fact* to 1. The ":=" means assignment. The next line is the first line of a loop which initializes *i* to 1 and adds 1 to it each time through the loop. *fact* is assigned the value *fact*∗*i* each time through the loop. When *i* = 10, the loop executes for the last time. A complete VAX-11 assembly language program to accomplish this is shown in Figure 1-2.

Understanding the factorial program

The factorial program contains comment statements:

> *Comment statements* begin with a ";". All characters following the ; until the end of the line are interpreted as a comment.

There are three labels in this program:

> *Labels* (also called *user-defined labels*) are symbolic names followed by a colon (:). For example, *result:* is a label.

In later sections, we will use another form of labels called local labels:

> *Local labels* are of the form "*n$:*", where $1 \leqslant n \leqslant 65535$. For example, *10$:* is a local label. Local labels are valid only until the next (or previous) user-defined label.

The instruction

```
movl #1,fact
```

initializes *fact* to 1 by putting the value 1 into the symbolic location *fact*. Then

Figure 1–2.

```
;
;This program calculates 10 factorial (10!)
;
fact:      .long
;
begin:     .word
           movl     #1,fact       ;  fact:=1
           movl     #1,r6         ;  i:=1
loop:      mull2    r6,fact       ;  fact:=fact*i
           aobleq   #10,r6,loop   ;  i:=i+1
           ret
           .end     begin
```

```
movl #1,r6
```

initializes Register 6 to 1. Note that Register 6 seems to be assuming the role played by i in the algorithm. The instruction

```
mull2 r6,fact
```

multiplies the contents of Register 6 by the contents of location *fact*. The instruction

```
aobleq #10,r6,loop
```

is read as "*add one* to Register 6 and *branch* to loop if it is *less* than or *equal* to 10." This instruction and the others in this chapter will be studied in greater detail in Chapter 4.

1.4 Pragmatics

Now that we have seen an assembly language program or two, it is time to consider how to enter such a program into the VAX-11 computer.

In the "old days"—10 years is old in the computer field—programs were punched onto cards. A few special cards called control cards were put at the beginning which identified the programmer and gave instructions to the computer. These computer systems were called batch systems, and many computers, including the VAX, can still be used this way.

The more common way of using the VAX and other modern computers is via time-sharing. In time-sharing, the programmer enters his or her program from a typewriter-like device called a terminal. The programmer is thus "sharing" the computer with all the people typing in from other terminals. Control cards are replaced by a *command language*. A command language is, as the name implies, a language of commands. The VAX operating system interprets these commands. The operating system thus acts as a "liaison" between the computer and the programs being run on the computer.

There are seven basic steps to entering and running a program on the VAX; each of these steps can be accomplished by typing in the appropriate command or commands. These steps are listed below and described in detail in Appendix A. Steps 0–4 and 6 are the usual steps on the VAX for entering and running any program in any language (BASIC, Pascal, FORTRAN, etc.). Step 5 is a useful method for debugging assembly language programs and for examining the contents of memory locations.

Step 0: Login—the term used to access the computer from a terminal.
Step 1: Edit—create and/or correct a program.

Step 2: Assemble—change the program from assembly language to machine language. If there are errors, return to step 1.

Step 3: Link—assign memory addresses to the assembled program. If there are errors, return to step 1.

Step 4: Run—execute the linked program. If there are errors, return to step 1.

Step 5: Debug—use the system debugger to examine the contents of memory locations. If there are errors, return to step 1.

Step 6: Logout—the term used to disconnect the terminal from the computer.

The reader is strongly urged at this time to become familiar with these operations. Appendix A describes them in detail and illustrates them for the two assembly language programs described in this chapter. By following the steps needed to run these programs, the reader will become familiar with the VAX/VMS operating system and the running of VAX assembly language programs. The rest of Part I is devoted to learning how to *write* VAX assembly language programs.

Getting comfortable

This chapter is introductory. It is also intended to be motivational. Right from the beginning, we have seen that we will need to become familiar with the VAX architecture, with the binary number system, and with the way data types (e.g., integers) are stored. Chapters 2 and 3 discuss these concepts. Chapter 4 then introduces the instruction set for the VAX assembly language.

Exercises

1. What are the symbols used in machine language, and what are they called?
2. What is the function of the assembler?
3. What are the two parts of an assembly language instruction, and what does each do?
4. Where is the address of the next executable instruction held?
5. Is an address represented by a bit pattern?
6. In the program that computes 10-factorial,
   a. What symbolic address contains the computed value 10-factorial?
   b. Where is the value of the counter i stored?
7. Write a single instruction to perform the following calculation: $b:=a^2$. *Note:* It is a variation of one of the instructions used in this chapter.
8. How many machine language instructions are generated for each assembly language instruction?
9. ; The following assembly language program
   ; finds the sum and average (when the
   ; sum is even!) of two 32-bit numbers:

```
    x:        .long     10
    y:        .long     20
  sum:        .long
  avg:        .long
begin:        .word
              movl      x,r5
              addl3     y,r5,sum      ; sum=x+y
              divl3     #2,sum,avg    ; avg=sum/2
              ret
              .end      begin
```

Follow steps 0–6 described in this chapter for your system. Use the system debugger to examine the contents of location *sum* and *avg* when the program is finished.

Chapter 2

Machine Organization: VAX Architecture

2.1 Introduction

The VAX-11 is an extension of Digital Equipment Corporation's PDP-11 family of minicomputers. VAX is an acronym for Virtual Address Extension and indicates that the VAX has expanded memory facilities over its predecessor, the PDP-11. In fact, there are about 4 billion possible storage locations on the VAX-11/780.

Computer architecture refers to the structure of a computer—in particular to the description of registers, memory, and the operations that take place on them.

Word length

Word length is the number of bits in a main register or memory location. Computers differ in their word lengths. The word length for the VAX's predecessor, the PDP-11, is 16 bits; the word length for the VAX is 32 bits.

Other differences in architecture

Computers also differ in other ways besides word length. They may differ in the number and uses of registers, in the amount of memory available, in the number and use of peripheral devices (disks, terminals, line printers, etc.), to name a few. In this chapter we will describe the architecture for the VAX. In particular, we will look at the different sizes of storage elements, the size, number and uses of registers, and the VAX address space.

2.2 Storage Elements

Bits

The smallest storage element of any computer is the *bit,* which can have a value of 0 or 1.

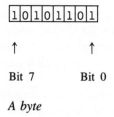

A bit

Clearly, a bit cannot represent much information. In fact, it can contain only one of two values—0 or 1. Thus we usually represent values in groups of consecutive bits called, on the VAX, bytes, words, longwords, and quadwords.

Bytes

The next larger size of information is a *byte,* which, for the VAX, is a sequence of 8 bits. The bits in a byte are numbered from right to left with the rightmost bit (called the least significant bit) numbered 0 and the leftmost bit (the most significant bit) numbered 7:

1	0	1	0	1	1	0	1

↑   ↑

Bit 7   Bit 0

A byte

Words

Larger-sized storage elements are now found by multiplying by 2. A *word* equals 2 bytes; thus a word consists of 16 bits. In this text, we will picture words in two different ways: (1) as a horizontal sequence of 16 bits and (2) as a vertical sequence of two bytes:

1	0	1	1	1	0	0	0	1	0	1	1	0	0	0	1

↑   ↑

Bit 15   Bit 0

A word written horizontally

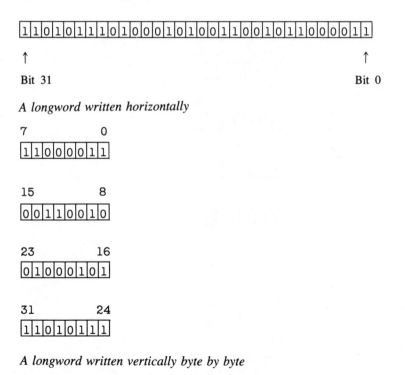

Bit 7   Bit 0

| 1 | 0 | 1 | 1 | 0 | 0 | 0 | 1 |

| 1 | 0 | 1 | 1 | 1 | 0 | 0 | 0 |

Bit 15   Bit 8

A word written vertically byte by byte

Longwords

Two words become a *longword*. These 32-bit longwords are frequently used to store addresses. Since each of the 32 bits may be either 0 or 1, there are thus 2^{32} addresses. Because of this 32-bit architecture, it is frequently, but ambiguously, said that the *word size* of the VAX is 32 bits:

| 1 | 1 | 0 | 1 | 0 | 1 | 1 | 1 | 0 | 1 | 0 | 0 | 0 | 1 | 0 | 1 | 0 | 0 | 1 | 1 | 0 | 0 | 1 | 0 | 1 | 1 | 0 | 0 | 0 | 0 | 1 | 1 |

Bit 31   Bit 0

A longword written horizontally

7   0

| 1 | 1 | 0 | 0 | 0 | 0 | 1 | 1 |

15   8

| 0 | 0 | 1 | 1 | 0 | 0 | 1 | 0 |

23   16

| 0 | 1 | 0 | 0 | 0 | 1 | 0 | 1 |

31   24

| 1 | 1 | 0 | 1 | 0 | 1 | 1 | 1 |

A longword written vertically byte by byte

```
15                          0
0 0 1 1 0 0 1 0 1 1 0 0 0 0 1 1
```

```
31                        16
1 1 0 0 1 1 1 1 0 1 0 0 0 1 0 1
```

A longword written as two consecutive words

Quadwords

The largest-size unit of information is called a *quadword*. A quadword is 2 longwords, hence 4 words or 8 bytes:

```
31                                                      0
0 1 0 1 0 1 0 1 0 1 0 1 0 1 0 1 0 1 0 1 0 1 0 1 0 1 0 1 0 1 0 1
```

```
0 1 0 1 0 1 0 1 0 1 0 1 0 1 0 1 0 1 0 1 0 1 0 1 0 1 0 1 0 1 0 1
63                                                     32
```

A quadword written as two consecutive longwords

```
7           0
0 1 0 1 0 1 0 1
```

```
15          8
0 1 0 1 0 1 0 1
```

```
23          16
0 1 0 1 0 1 0 1
```

```
31          24
0 1 0 1 0 1 0 1
```

```
39          32
0 1 0 1 0 1 0 1
```

```
47          40
0 1 0 1 0 1 0 1
```

```
55          48
0 1 0 1 0 1 0 1
```

```
63            56
0 1 0 1 0 1 0 1
```

A quadword written vertically byte by byte

Data storage

Bits, bytes, words, longwords, and quadwords are units of storage. They do not indicate what sort of data are stored in them. In the next chapter, we shall see that bytes, words, and longwords are frequently used to store integers. Certainly, the larger the storage unit, the larger the integer that can be stored there. In addition, we will see that longwords are large enough to store many decimal point numbers, although larger ("double-precision") decimal point numbers may require a quadword size of storage.

And finally, we will see that a byte is large enough to store characters (e.g., letters).

2.3   Memory

Computer memory consists of an ordered sequence of storage units, each with its own address. VAX memory is byte-addressable, which means that each byte has its own address. Thus, if *a* is the address of a longword, *a* is actually the address of the first byte of the longword. Then, *a+1* is the address of the second byte of the longword, and so on. This is one of the reasons why words, longwords, and quadwords were shown in the previous section as sequences of bytes.

Although we refer to memory locations symbolically (e.g., *a*), the VAX refers to each by a number. Thus the address we know of as *a* may, in reality, be address 207. The designers of the VAX specified that an address be representable by up to 32 bits. Thus the first address in memory is numbered 0 and the last address is numbered 11111111111111111111111111111111:

VAX-11 memory

Address	Example contents
00000000000000000000000000000000	11010000
00000000000000000000000000000001	00000010
00000000000000000000000000000010	01010110
.	.
.	.
.	.
11111111111111111111111111111111	00000000

Thus, there are 2^{32} addresses, hence 2^{32} memory locations (bytes). The combination of symbolic addresses and their contents is called the *address space*. The combination of the actual memory locations and their contents is called the *memory space*.

The stack

There is a block of memory locations automatically reserved called the stack, and one of the 16 general registers described below, R14, contains the address of the top of stack. Stacks will be described and used in Chapter 7.

2.4 Registers

The VAX-11 has 16 registers referred to as R0, R1, . . . , R15. Each of these registers is 32 bits long. Thus, among other things, a register is large enough to hold an address.

Four of these registers are used for special purposes as described in the following paragraphs.

The program counter

R15 is the program counter (PC). It contains the address of the next instruction to be executed. When the CPU has finished executing one instruction, the contents of the PC are consulted to find the location of the next instruction to execute. The PC is then updated (by the computer) to contain the location of the next instruction. The VAX does this by adding the amount of memory occupied by the instruction to the present contents of the PC. After this is done, the PC once again contains the location of the next instruction to execute.

The stack pointer

R14 (also denoted SP for stack pointer) contains the address of the area of memory known as the system stack. The stack and the SP are discussed in Chapter 7.

The frame pointer

R13 (also denoted FP for frame pointer) contains the address of information automatically pushed onto the stack as a result of a procedure call. Procedures and procedure calls are discussed in Chapter 7.

The argument pointer

R12 (also denoted AP for argument pointer) contains the address of the first argument in a procedure call. We will discuss the AP extensively in Chapter 7.

Other registers

Registers 6 through 11 have no special significance and can be used freely by the programmer. Registers 0 through 5 usually have no special significance; there are some instructions (e.g., the character string instructions discussed in Chapter 9), however, that do alter the contents of these registers. The programmer is free to use registers 0 through 5 but should do so carefully.

Registers are high-speed storage locations. They are used for holding temporary values, for performing arithmetic operations, for holding addresses of data, and for indexing arrays. They are also expensive to build with today's technology, which is why there are not 2^{32} of them!

The processor status longword

In addition to registers R0 through R15, there is a group of 32 bits called the processor status longword (PSL). The most important (to us) of these bits, bits 0–3, called C, V, Z, and N, respectively, are called *condition codes* and contain information during execution about the last executed instruction:

EXAMPLE

```
                                                   N Z V C
┌──┬──┬──┬──┬──┬──┬──┬──┬──┬──┬──┬──┬──┬──┬──┬──┬──┬──┬──┬──┬──┬──┬──┬──┬──┬──┬──┬──┬┬──┬──┬──┐
│  │  │  │  │  │  │  │  │  │  │  │  │  │  │  │  │  │  │  │  │  │  │  │  │  │  │  │  ││1 │0 │0 │1 │
└──┴──┴──┴──┴──┴──┴──┴──┴──┴──┴──┴──┴──┴──┴──┴──┴──┴──┴──┴──┴──┴──┴──┴──┴──┴──┴──┴──┴┴──┴──┴──┘
```

PSL

These bits are said to be *set* if they contain a 1 and *cleared* if they contain a 0. Many assembly language instructions affect the condition codes in some way. *Movl,* for example, clears V; it sets N to 1 if the quantity moved is negative; otherwise it clears N. Similarly, the Z bit is set if the quantity moved is 0; otherwise, Z is cleared. The C bit is not changed.

In general, the N bit is set by instructions storing *negative* quantities and cleared by instructions storing positive quantities or 0. The Z bit is set by instructions storing the quantity zero; otherwise, it is cleared. The V bit (for *overflow*) is set by arithmetic instructions whose results do not fit into the designated storage unit. Similarly, the C bit is set by unsigned arithmetic instructions which involve a carryout of or a borrow into the most significant bit. We will use condition codes when describing the branch instructions in Chapter 4.

The registers and the PSL are part of the VAX's central processing unit (CPU). The CPU retrieves information from memory and determines what operations to perform and when.

Exercises

1. What does VAX stand for, and what does it mean?

2. Memory addresses are how many bits long? How many locations does this allow for? What is referenced by an address?

3. Fill in the chart:

Storage element	Size in bits	Largest unsigned integer that can occupy this element
Byte	10	
Word	26	2^64
Longword	32	2
Quadword	64	

4. Which register contains the address of the top of the stack?

5. Give the alternate names for R12, R13, R14, and R15.

6. What is the advantage of having a 32-bit architecture (as in the VAX) over a 16-bit architecture (as in the PDP-11)?

7.
```
;The following assembly language program
;is the same as the program in
;exercise 9 of Chapter 1 except
;that instead of using longword
;storage elements, word storage
;elements are used:

   x:     .word    10     ; x=10
   y:     .word    20     ; y=20
 sum:     .word
 avg:     .word
begin:    .word
          movw     x,r5
          addw3    y,r5,sum    ; sum=x+y
          divw3    #2,sum,avg  ; avg=sum/2
          ret
          .end     begin
```

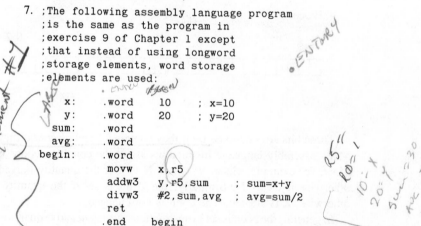

Follow Steps 0–6 from Chapter 1. Use the system debugger to examine the contents of location *sum* and *avg*. (You will need to say "set type word" in most versions of VMS.)

DUE FRIDAY
W/ CHANGES
.LIST & DEBUG RUN
ANOTHER REASON WHY THEY CALL IT DOPE!
PFCA
BUD

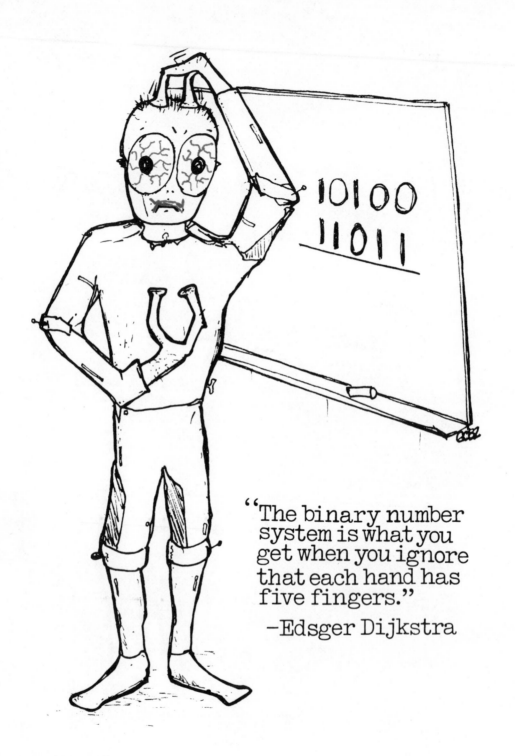

Chapter 3

Representation of Data

3.1 Binary, Decimal, and Hexadecimal Numbers

Introduction

Although the computer does its work in binary, it is more convenient for us to look at these calculations in hexadecimal (base 16). There are three reasons for this:

1. Binary machine code is usually long and difficult to assimilate. Hexadecimal is much easier to read.
2. There is a one-to-one correspondence between binary and hexadecimal. Thus it is easy to translate from the hexadecimal to binary.
3. VAX storage elements are multiples or fractions of 16. Thus it is convenient to show contents as multiples and fractions of 16 (hexadecimal). This is clear from the discussion of storage elements in Chapter 2. There, we saw that storage sizes were 8 bits (a byte), 16 bits (a word), 32 bits (a longword), and 64 bits (a quadword).

The remainder of this section discusses the binary, hexadecimal, and decimal number systems and the methods for converting from one number system to another. Readers comfortable with these concepts might like to go directly to Section 3.2.

Conversions

To see the one-to-one correspondence between hexadecimal and binary, note that if $b_n b_{n-1} \ldots b_1 b_0$ is a binary number x, then (reading from right to left):

$$\cdots\ +\ 2^9 b_9\ +2^8 b_8\ +2^7 b_7\ +2^6 b_6\ +2^5 b_5\ +2^4 b_4\ +2^3 b_3\ +2^2 b_2\ +2^1 b_1\ +b_0 = x$$

$$\cdots\ +\ 512 b_9\ +256 b_8\ +128 b_7\ +64 b_6\ +32 b_5\ +16 b_4\ +8 b_3\ +4 b_2\ +2 b_1\ +b_0 = x$$

$$\cdots\ +\ 2 b_9\ \ \ +1 b_8)\ \ \times 16^2\ \ \ +(8 b_7\ +4 b_6\ \ +2 b_5\ \ +1 b_4) \times 16^1$$
$$+\ (8 b_3 + 4 b_2 + 2 b_1 + 1 b_0) \times 16^0 = x$$

Each of the sums in parentheses is a number between 0 (if all the b_i values are 0) and 15 (if all the b_i values are 1). These are exactly the *digits* in the hexadecimal number system; see Figure 3–1. Thus, to convert from binary to hexadecimal, "gather up" groups of 4.

EXAMPLE

Convert the VAX word 0010101100111000 to hexadecimal.
Solution:

0010101100111000

2   B   3   8

That is, $0010101100111000_2 = 2B38_{16}$.

Converting hexadecimal to binary is the opposite process:

Figure 3–1.

Binary	Decimal	Hexadecimal
1	1	1
10	2	2
11	3	3
100	4	4
101	5	5
110	6	6
111	7	7
1000	8	8
1001	9	9
1010	10	A
1011	11	B
1100	12	C
1101	13	D
1110	14	E
1111	15	F
10000	16	10
10001	17	11
.	.	.
.	.	.
.	.	.

EXAMPLE
Convert D0 to binary.
Solution:

D   0
$\overbrace{}\,\overbrace{}$
11010000

That is, $D0_{16} = 11010000_2$.

The other conversions we will need to perform fairly fluently are binary to decimal, decimal to binary, decimal to hexadecimal, and hexadecimal to decimal.

Binary to decimal conversions

Method. Write the binary sequence in its place-value summation form and then evaluate.

EXAMPLE
$$
\begin{aligned}
10101010 &= 1 \times 2^7 + 0 \times 2^6 + 1 \times 2^5 + 0 \times 2^4 + 1 \times 2^3 + 0 \times 2^2 \\
&\quad + 1 \times 2^1 + 0 \times 2^0 \\
&= 2^7 + 2^5 + 2^3 + 2^1 \\
&= 128 + 32 + 8 + 2 \\
&= 170
\end{aligned}
$$

Decimal to binary conversions

Method 1. Use a table of powers of 2 to reduce the decimal sequence to a summation of powers of 2; see Figure 3–2.

Figure 3–2. *Powers of 2*

n	2^n
0	1
1	2
2	4
3	8
4	16
5	32
6	64
7	128
8	256
.	.
.	.
.	.

EXAMPLE

$345_{10} = 2^8 + 89 \qquad (2^9 \text{ is larger than } 345)$

$= 2^8 + 2^6 + 25$

$= 2^8 + 2^6 + 2^4 + 9$

$= 2^8 + 2^6 + 2^4 + 2^3 + 1$

$= 2^8 + 2^6 + 2^4 + 2^3 + 2^0$

$= 1 \times 2^8 + 0 \times + 2^7 + 1 \times 2^6 + 0 \times 2^5 + 1 \times 2^4 + 1 \times 2^3 + 0 \times 2^2$
$+ 0 \times 2^1 + 1 \times 2^0$

$= 101011001_2$

Method 2. Divide the decimal number successively by 2; remainders are the coefficients of 2^0, 2^1, 2^2, ...

EXAMPLE

$345/2 = 172,$ remainder 1; coefficient of 2^0 is 1

$172/2 = 86,$ remainder 0; coefficient of 2^1 is 0

$86/2 = 43,$ remainder 0; coefficient of 2^2 is 0

$43/2 = 21,$ remainder 1; coefficient of 2^3 is 1

$21/2 = 10;$ remainder 1; coefficient of 2^4 is 1

$10/2 = 5;$ remainder 0; coefficient of 2^5 if 0

$5/2 = 2;$ remainder 1; coefficient of 2^6 is 1

$2/2 = 1,$ remainder 0; coefficient of 2^7 is 0

$1/2 = 0,$ remainder 1; coefficient of 2^8 is 1

Thus, $345_{10} = 101011001_2$.

This works because we want to find the coefficients $b_0, b_1, b_2, \ldots$ (which are 0 or 1) of 2^0, 2^1, 2^2, . . . , and so on. Thus

$$345 = b_{10}2^{10} + b_9 2^9 + b_8 2^8 + \ldots + b_1 2^1 + b_0 2^0$$

Dividing by 2,

$$345/2 = b_{10}2^9 + b_9 2^8 + \ldots + b_1 + (b_0/2)$$

Thus b_0 is the remainder on division by 2 and $(b_{10}2^9 + b_9 2^8 + \ldots + b_1)$ is the quotient.

Decimal to hexadecimal conversions

Method 1. Use a table of powers of 16 to reduce the decimal sequence to a summation of powers of 16; see Figure 3–3.

EXAMPLE

$302_{10} = 1 \times 16^2 + 46 \qquad (16^3 \text{ is greater than } 302)$

$= 1 \times 16^2 + 2 \times 16^1 + 14$

$= 1 \times 16^2 + 2 \times 16^1 + E \times 16^0 \qquad (14_{10} = E_{16})$

$= 12E_{16}$

Figure 3–3. *Powers of 16*

n	16
0	1
1	16
2	256
3	4096
4	65536
5	1048576
6	16777216
7	268435456
8	4294967296
9	68719476736
10	1099511627776
11	17592186044416
.	.
.	.
.	.

Method 2. Divide the decimal number successively by 16; remainders are the coefficients of 16^0, 16^1, 16^2, ...

EXAMPLE
302/16 = 18,   remainder 14; coefficient of 16^0 is E
18/16 = 1,   remainder 2; coefficient of 16^1 is 2
1/16 = 0,   remainder 1; coefficient of 16^2 is 1

Therefore, $302_{10} = 12E_{16}$.

This works for the same reason that method 2 for decimal-to-binary (above) works. That is, division by 16 produces as a remainder the coefficient (h_0) of 16^0, and as a quotient the decimal number minus the quantity ($h_0 \times 16^0$).

Hexadecimal to decimal conversions

Method. Write the hexadecimal number in its place-value summation form and then evaluate.

EXAMPLE
$$CA14_{16} = C \times 16^3 + A \times 16^2 + 1 \times 16^1 + 4 \times 16^0$$
$$= 12 \times 4096 + 10 \times 256 + 16 + 4$$
$$= 51732_{10}$$

Converting binary fractions to decimal

Method. Binary fractions are easy to understand if we remember what the place-value summation form of a decimal fraction is. For example,

$$.237_{10} = 2 \times 10^{-1} + 3 \times 10^{-2} + 7 \times 10^{-3}$$

Similarly,

$$.1011_2 = 1 \times 2^{-1} + 0 \times 2^{-2} + 1 \times 2^{-3} + 1 \times 2^{-4}$$

Evaluating this summation form changes the binary fraction to a decimal fraction.

EXAMPLE
Convert $.1011_2$ to a decimal fraction.

$$.1011_2 = 1 \times 2^{-1} + 0 \times 2^{-2} + 1 \times 2^{-3} + 1 \times 2^{-4}$$
$$= 1/2 + 1/8 + 1/16 = 11/16 = .6875_{10}$$

Converting decimal fractions to binary

Method. Multiply the decimal fraction successively by 2; the integer parts of the result are the coefficients of 2^{-1}, 2^{-2}, 2^{-3}, ...

EXAMPLE
.6875 × 2 = 1.3750;   integer part is 1; coefficient of 2^{-1} is 1
.3750 × 2 = 0.7500;   integer part is 0; coefficient of 2^{-2} is 0
.7500 × 2 = 1.5000;   integer part is 1; coefficient of 2^{-3} is 1
.5000 × 2 = 1.0000;   integer part is 1; coefficient of 2^{-4} is 1

Thus,

$$.6875_{10} = .1011_2$$

Arithmetic

Doing arithmetic in the binary and hexadecimal number systems is best shown by examples and best learned by practice. (It sometimes helps to do a few similar decimal examples slowly.)

EXAMPLE

```
  1011
+1001
------
 10100
```

(*Remember:* 1 + 1 is 0 with a 1 "carry.")

EXAMPLE

```
 1110
- 101
-----
 1001
```

(*Remember:* To subtract 1 from 0, borrow a 1 from the place to the left; it becomes a 10_2 (=2_{10}) when moved to the right.)

EXAMPLE

$$\begin{array}{r} 1A \\ +\ 5 \\ \hline 1F \end{array}$$

(In decimal, A + 5 is 10 + 5 = 15; $15_{10} = F_{16}$.)

EXAMPLE

$$\begin{array}{r} FF \\ +\ \ 3 \\ \hline 102 \end{array}$$

(F + 3 is 15 + 3 in decimal; $18_{10} = 12_{16}$, so we write down a 2, carry 1.)

EXAMPLE

$$\begin{array}{r} 13 \\ -A \\ \hline 9 \end{array}$$

(Borrow 1 from the 1; it becomes a $10_{16} = 16_{10}$ when moved to the right. In decimal, 16 + 3 = 19 and 19 – 10 = 9.)

We encourage the reader to become familiar with the three number systems and adept at converting from one to another.

In the remainder of this chapter, we will learn how the VAX stores

1. Positive and negative integers
2. Floating point numbers
3. Letters and other characters

3.2 Representing Positive and Negative Integers

We can easily see how positive integers are stored. For example, 345 is stored as 101011001. This will not fit into a byte (why not?), but fits easily into a word (two consecutive bytes).

EXAMPLE
Show 65712_{10} as a binary

(a) byte,   (b) word,   (c) longword,   (d) quadword.

$65712_{10} = 10000000010110000_2$

Solution:
(a) Does not fit in a byte

(b) Does not fit in a word

(c) 00000000000000010000000010110000

(d) 00000000000000010000000010110000
     00000000000000000000000000000000

Storing negative integers presents a more difficult problem since the negative sign has to be represented (by a 0 or a 1) or some indication must be made (in binary!) that the integer is negative. Historically, many different methods have been used. We will discuss three of these here: (1) sign and magnitude, (2) one's complement, and (3) two's complement.

Sign and magnitude. This is the simplest method. Knuth used sign and magnitude in his mythical MIX computer. In sign-and-magnitude representation of signed integers, the leftmost (most significant) bit represents the sign—0 for positive, 1 for negative.

EXAMPLE
31 stored in a byte using sign-and-magnitude representation:

00011111

↑   31
Positive

−31 becomes

10011111

↑   31
Negative

There are two drawbacks to sign-and-magnitude representation of signed integers:

1. There are two representations of 0 (what are they?). Thus the CPU has to make two checks every time it tests for 0 since it must test for both +0 and −0.
2. $a + (-b)$ is not the same is $a - b$. Thus, the logic designer must build separate circuits for subtracting; the adding circuit used for $a + b$ is not sufficient.

EXAMPLE
Show that $52 - 31$ and $52 + (-31)$ are not the same in sign and magnitude representation.

$$
\begin{array}{rcl}
52 & = & 00110100 \\
-31 & = & -00011111 \\
\hline
21 & = & 00010101
\end{array}
\qquad
\begin{array}{rcl}
52 & = & 00110100 \\
+{-31} & = & -10011111 \\
\hline
21 & \neq & 11010011
\end{array}
$$

One's complement. This method of storing signed integers is used in Control Data Corporation's 6000 and Cyber 70 Series of computers. In one's complement, the leftmost bit is still 0 for a positive integer. For example, 00011111 still represents +31. To form the negative, however, we replace all 0's by 1's and all 1's by 0's. Thus, −31 becomes 11100000. Note that the leftmost bit of negative integers is again 1.

EXAMPLE
Store −31 in a word of storage using one's complement.
  Solution: 31 as a word is 0000000000011111, so that −31 as a word is 1111111111100000.

The second drawback to sign and magnitude has been eliminated: $a + (-b) = a - b$. Thus the circuit designer need only include an adder, since this adder can also be used for subtraction. The following example shows that this adder must do a little more than just "add."

EXAMPLE
Show that $52 - 31$ and $52 + (-31)$ are the same in one's complement representation.
  Solution:

$$
\begin{array}{rcl}
52 & = & 00110100 \\
-31 & = & -00011111 \\
\hline
21 & = & 00010101
\end{array}
\qquad
\begin{array}{rcl}
52 & = & 00110100 \\
+{-31} & = & +11100000 \\
\hline
 & & 100010100 \\
\end{array}
$$

$$
\begin{array}{rcl}
 & & \llcorner \longrightarrow +1 \\
\hline
21 & = & 00010101
\end{array}
$$

Notice that the "adder" must carry around any overflow bit in order to work correctly for subtraction. The first drawback is still with us, however: there are still two representations of 0 (what are they?). We are thus led to the following.

Two's complement. This method of storing signed integers is used in the VAX computer and the IBM 360/370, to name just two. The two's complement is formed by (a) forming the one's complement and then (b) adding 1.

EXAMPLE
31 is (still) stored in a byte as 00011111.

$$
\begin{array}{ll}
- \, 31 \text{ becomes} & 11100000 \\
& +1 \\
\hline
& 11100001
\end{array}
$$

$$
\begin{array}{ll}
-(-31) \text{ becomes} & 00011110 \\
& +1 \\
\hline
& 00011111 \quad \text{as it should be.}
\end{array}
$$

The reader can check that, once again, $a + (-b)$ has the same answer as $a - b$ and that there is only one representation of 0.

3.3   Representing Floating-Point Numbers

Storing floating-point numbers presents a problem similar to that in Section 3.2 of storing signed integers. There, some indication of a negative or positive sign had to be represented; here, some method must be devised for showing where the decimal point should go. Again, different methods have been used in the past. We will describe here only the method used in the VAX. Similar methods are used in most of today's computers.

The first step to seeing how a binary fraction is stored in memory is to normalize it, that is, to write it so that the first digit after the point is 1.

EXAMPLE
Normalize 0.000111101.
Solution: $0.000111101 = 0.111101 \times 2^{-3}$

Then store this normalized fraction into a (32-bit) longword: Store the rightmost 7 bits of the fraction into the rightmost 7 bits of the longword. Store the exponent into bits 7–14 of the longword. Store the sign of the floating-point number (0 for positive, 1 for negative) into bit 15 of the longword. Store the remaining fractional part, if any, into bits 16–31 left-adjusted. Two final adjustments are made before the fraction is stored:

1. Since the fraction is normalized, we know that the first digit after the point is 1. This is remembered and not stored. (Computer designers do not waste a bit!).
2. Since bits 7–14 represent the exponent, only exponents from 1 to 255 could be represented; in particular, this would not allow negative exponents. So before the exponent is stored, 128 (= 10000000_2) is added to it. Now exponents from –127 to 127 can be stored.

EXAMPLE

Show $.111101 \times 2^{-3}$ as the VAX would store it.

Solution: The exponent is $128 + (-3) = 125 = 01111101_2$. The fraction (minus the first 1 after the point) = .11101. The floating-point number is stored as:

Exponent   Fraction

00000000000000000$\overbrace{0111110}$$\overbrace{11110100}$

Rest of fraction   Sign

EXAMPLE

What floating point number is stored in the VAX as

000000000000000000011111000100000?

Solution: The exponent is $01111100_2 = 124_{10}$. Since 128 was added to it, the original exponent must be –4. The fraction is 0100000, but remember that the first 1 after the decimal point is not stored. Thus the fraction is .10100000. The floating-point number is thus

$$.10100000 \times 2^{-4} = (1 \times 2^{-1} + 0 \times 2^{-2} + 1 \times 2^{-3}) \times 2^{-4}$$
$$= 0.0390625_{10}$$

3.4   Representing Characters

This section considers the problem of storing characters (in particular, letters). The possible characters include

Letters:	A, B, . . . , Z, a, b, . . . , z
Digits:	0, 1, . . . , 9
Special characters:	+, –, *, /, \$, etc.
Nonprinting characters:	bell, linefeed (LF), carriage return (CR), etc.

Counting up all the possible characters, we discover that there are fewer than 128. Thus if we code carefully, a byte will be more than large enough to represent any character.

There have been many methods devised for storing characters. The VAX uses a code called ASCII, which stands for American Standard Code for Information Interchange. Figure 3-4 shows the ASCII codes for the various characters. They are shown in hexadecimal for the usual reasons. Note that the ASCII code for the digit i is $30 + i$. We will not define the "meaning" of the nonprinting characters in column 1 (see hex 0–1F). The interested reader can find their meaning in the *VAX-11 MACRO Language Reference Manual* [18].
The character $\char`\^$ indicates use of the control key.

EXAMPLE
The character A is stored in the VAX as 41_{16} ($=01000001_2$).

EXAMPLE
VAX-11 is stored in the VAX as

$$
\begin{array}{c}
56 \\
41 \\
58 \\
2D \\
31 \\
31
\end{array}
$$

3.5   Data Storage Directives

Assembler directives are instructions to the assembler; they are not necessarily translated into machine language. In appearance, they look very much like assembly language instructions except that they begin with a ".".

EXAMPLE

```
    end start
```

informs the assembler that this is the end of the program whose beginning is at the location whose symbolic name is *start*.

This section will discuss those assembler directives which reserve, reference, and initialize various-sized memory locations. Data storage directives exist for all the previously described data types, as well as for some not mentioned in this text.

Allocating memory

The following are used to allot and initialize a small number of memory locations:

```
.byte .word .long .quad .float .ascii
.asciz .ascic .address
```

Figure 3–4. *Diablo 1640 keyboard*

The character ^ indicates use of the control key.

DEC	OCT	HEX	NAME	KEY	DEC	OCT	HEX	KEY	DEC	OCT	HEX	KEY
000	000	00	NUL	^@	043	053	2B	+	086	126	56	V
001	001	01	SOH	^A	044	054	2C	'	087	127	57	W
002	002	02	STX	^B	045	055	2D	–	088	130	58	X
003	003	03	ETX	^C	046	056	2E	.	089	131	59	Y
004	004	04	EOT	^D	047	057	2F	/	090	132	5A	Z
005	005	05	ENQ	^E	048	060	30	0	091	133	5B	[
006	006	06	ACK	^F	049	061	31	1	092	134	5C	\
007	007	07	BEL	^G	050	062	32	2	093	135	5D	]
008	010	08	BS	^H	051	063	33	3	094	136	5E	^
009	011	09	HT	^I/TAB	052	064	34	4	095	137	5F	_
010	012	0A	LF	^J/LF	053	065	35	5	096	140	60	`
011	013	0B	VT	^K	054	066	36	6	097	141	61	a
012	014	0C	FF	^L	055	067	37	7	098	142	62	b
013	015	0D	CR	^M/CR	056	070	38	8	099	143	63	c
014	016	0E	SO	^N	057	071	39	9	100	144	64	d
015	017	0F	SI	^O	058	072	3A	:	101	145	65	e
016	020	10	DLE	^P	059	073	3B	;	102	146	66	f
017	021	11	DC1	^Q	060	074	3C	<	103	147	67	g
018	022	12	DC2	^R	061	075	3D	=	104	150	68	h
019	023	13	DC3	^S	062	076	3E	>	105	151	69	i
020	024	14	DC4	^T	063	077	3F	?	106	152	6A	j
021	025	15	NAK	^U	064	100	40	@	107	153	6B	k
022	026	16	SYN	^V	065	101	41	A	108	154	6C	l
023	027	17	ETB	^W	066	102	42	B	109	155	6D	m
024	030	18	CAN	^X	067	103	43	C	110	156	6E	n
025	031	19	EM	^Y	068	104	44	D	111	157	6F	o
026	032	1A	SUB	^Z	069	105	45	E	112	160	70	p
027	033	1B	ESC	ESC	070	106	46	F	113	161	71	q
028	034	1C	FS	^\	071	107	47	G	114	162	72	r
029	035	1D	GS	^]	072	110	48	H	115	163	73	s
030	036	1E	RS	^^	073	111	49	I	116	164	74	t
031	037	1F	US	^	074	112	4A	J	117	165	75	u
032	040	20	SP	SPACE	075	113	4B	K	118	166	76	v
033	041	21		!	076	114	4C	L	119	167	77	w
034	042	22		"	077	115	4D	M	120	170	78	x
035	043	23		#	078	116	4E	N	121	171	79	y
036	044	24		$	079	117	4F	O	122	172	7A	z
037	045	25		%	080	120	50	P	123	173	7B	{
038	046	26		&	081	121	51	Q	124	174	7C		
039	047	27		'	082	122	52	R	125	175	7D	}
040	050	28		(	083	123	53	S	126	176	7E	~
041	051	29		)	084	124	54	T	127	177	7F	DEL
042	052	2A		*	085	125	55	U				

EXAMPLE

```
a: .long 2
```

stores the integer 2 into 4 consecutive bytes whose address is *a*.

EXAMPLE

```
input: .word 20, 23, 102, −76, 0
```

allots consecutive 16-bit words containing 20, 23, 102, −76, and 0. The address of the first word (whose contents is 20) is *input*. Then 23 is stored at *input + 2* (bytes) since a word is two bytes.

EXAMPLE

```
list: .byte 1[10]
```

initializes an array of 10 bytes to the value 1. This bracketed repeat factor cannot be used with the block storage directives below.

EXAMPLE

```
pi: .float 3.14159
```

sets aside a longword whose first byte is address *pi* and initializes this longword to 3.14159.

Allocating larger amounts of memory

To allot and/or initialize larger amounts of memory space, use

```
.blkb, .blkw, .blkl, .blkq, .blkf, .blka
```

denoting a block of bytes, words, longwords, quadwords, floating-point numbers, and addresses, respectively. Remember that longwords, floating-point numbers, and addresses all occupy 32 bits.

EXAMPLE

```
output: .blkw 10
```

A block of 10 words is reserved whose first word is at the symbolic location *output*.

.ascii, .asciz, .ascic

.ascii is used for storing a group of characters in consecutive bytes. *.asciz* does the same, but appends a 0 for the last byte as an end marker. And *.ascic* is the same

as *.ascii* except that the first byte contains a count of the number of characters in the string. The ASCII characters must be enclosed by identical characters which do not themselves occur in the string. Slashes or quotes are used most frequently.

EXAMPLE

```
string1:   .ascii  /hello/
string2:   .asciz  /hello/
string3:   .ascic  /hello/
```

generates the following machine code written in hexadecimal from right to left:

```
   6F 6C 6C 65 68   string1: .ascii /hello/
00 6F 6C 6C 65 68   string2: .asciz /hello/
   6F 6C 6C 65 68 00' string3: .ascic /hello/
                05
```

Consulting the ASCII chart (Figure 3–4), we see that 68 is the code (in hex) for *h*, 65 is the code for *e*, and so forth. (The 05 is in the location initially marked 00'—the assembler has to translate all the characters before it knows there are 5!)

3.6 Assembler Symbols

The VAX-11 assembler assigns a special meaning to the symbols "^", "#", "=", and ".".

The symbol ^

The assembler assumes that the number we write in our assembly language programs are in decimal. Thus

```
a: .byte 10
```

initializes address *a* to 10_{10}. But we may use numbers in binary, octal, and hexadecimal by preceding them with ^B, ^O, and ^X, respectively. Thus

```
b: .byte ^B10
```

initializes *b* to $10_2 = 2_{10}$. (We capitalize the "B" since on our—and most—keyboards "^" is uppercase, i.e., we have to use the shift key for "^"—we might as well use it for "B" also. The "^" key on some keyboards is the up-arrow, " ↑ ".) And

```
c: .byte ^O10
```

initializes c to $10_8 = 8_{10}$. And

    d: .byte ^X10

initializes d to $10_{16} = 16_{10}$. Of course, other storage sizes like .word, .long, and so on may also be used.

Single characters may be stored by using ^A and .byte (since each ASCII character occupies one byte). Thus

    string4: .byte ^A/h/

generates the machine code 68. Similarly,

    pi: .long ^F3.14159

produces the same machine code as *pi: .float 3.14159*.

The symbol

The character # indicates that what follows is a *constant* or *literal* (constant expression).

EXAMPLE

    movl #1,r6

puts a copy of the constant 1 into Register 6.

Constants may be used in conjunction with ^:

EXAMPLE

    movl #^F3.14159,r6

Here, a copy of the constant 3.14159 is put into Register 6.

EXAMPLE

    movq #^A/hello/,r6

puts the characters *hell* into Register 6. The remaining character, *o* is put into the rightmost byte of the next register, Register 7.

The symbol =

In VAX assembly language, the symbol "=" assigns a value to a variable *during assembly*. Thus

    a=2

assigns the value 2 to the variable *a* during assembly. No memory location is assigned to *a*. *During execution*, symbols whose values were assigned by = during assembly are considered constants; they should be preceded by "#".

EXAMPLE

```
movl #a,r6
```

copies the value assigned to the symbol *a* (by =) into Register 6.

EXAMPLE

```
pi=^F3.14159
        .
        .
        .
start:    .word
        .
        .
        .
        movl        #pi,r6
```

copies the constant 3.14159 into Register 6.

The symbol .

Assembly is the process of translating an assembly language program into machine code. This machine code is stored into consecutive byte locations. The assembler assumes that the machine code is to be stored beginning at location 0. For example,

```
list: .byte 5,4,3,10,2
```

produces the following machine code:

Machine code	Location	Assembly language
02 0A 03 04 05	0000 0005	list: .byte 5,4,3,10,2

During assembly, the assembler maintains a *location counter* which contains the location (relative to 0) of the current byte of machine code being generated. Thus, when the fourth number in *list* is being translated into machine code, the location counter has a value of 3. After the machine code for the numbers in *list* has been generated, the next line will start with a location counter value of 0005.

The period "." has the current value of the location counter. The programmer may use this symbol in an assembly language program.

EXAMPLE

```
list: .byte 5,4,3,10,2
here=.
```

assigns the location counter value (5) to the constant *here*.

Arithmetic may be done during assembly by using the standard symbols $+$, $-$, $*$, and $/$. Angle brackets ($< >$) are used instead of parentheses.

EXAMPLE

```
list: .byte 5,4,3,10,2
count=.-list
```

assigns the value of the location counter (5) minus the location counter value for *list* (0 if this is the first instruction) to the constant *count*. That is, *count* is assigned the value 5.

EXAMPLE

```
list: .long 5,4,3,10,2
count=<.-list>/4
```

again assigns the value 5 to *count*. (Each of the numbers 5, 4, 3, 10, and 2 occupies 4 bytes.)

3.7 Machine Code

Figure 3–5 is the assembler output of the program from Chapter 1 which calculates $a*b+c$ when $a = 2$, $b = 3$, and $c = 4$.

It shows the machine code, location counter, and source program.

Remember that the location counter is initially set to 0 and the assembler generates the machine code into consecutive byte locations. The location counter always contains the location of the next byte.

EXAMPLE (from Figure 3–5, line 6)

Machine code	Location counter	Assembly language
56 EB AF D0	0012	movl a,r6
	0016	

Figure 3–5.

```
          00000002  0000   1 a:       .long  2
          00000003  0004   2 b:       .long  3
          00000004  0008   3 c:       .long  4
          00000000  000C   4 result:  .long
                    0010   5 start:   .word
       56 EB AF DO  0012   6          movl   a,r6
       56 EB AF C4  0016   7          mull2  b,r6
 EC AF 56 EB AF C1  001A   8          addl3  c,r6,result
                04  0020   9 last:    ret
                    0021  10          .end   start
```

Since the machine code (56 EB AF D0) occupies 4 bytes, 4 is added to the location counter. Thus the location counter is set to 0016 at the beginning of the next line. This machine code listing will be reexamined in Chapter 4 after a discussion of addressing modes and the instruction set. In particular, we will see why R6 is 56 in machine code, and why *a* translates into "EB AF".

Exercises

1. Why is hexadecimal a convenient number system for representing VAX machine code?
2. Convert the following binary numbers to hexadecimal:
   a. 0110111100111101
   b. 1011010011110101
   c. 11001010
   d. 11001
3. Convert the following hexadecimal numbers to binary:
   a. 8C4E
   b. F5
   c. 56
4. Using a byte storage element, show the two sign-and-magnitude representations of 0.
5. Using a byte storage element, show the two one's complement representations of 0.
6. Convert 127_{10} to binary.
7. Show how the VAX would store -53_{10}.
8. What negative number is represented in the VAX by 11111110?
9. Fill in the following hexadecimal multiplication table:

×	1	2	3	4	5	6	7	8	9	A
1										
2										
3										
4										
5										
6										
7										
8										
9										
A										

10. What floating point number is stored below?

    00000000000000011001110001000001

11. Show the hexadecimal ASCII code for *ascii*.

12. Is "b" less than "B"?

13. Write a storage directive which will initialize memory location *k* to the byte integer 12.

14. Which data storage directive would be used to reserve six consecutive bytes in memory starting at location *list*?

15. Given the following instruction

    ```
    input: .word 5,10,15,20,25
    ```

    and that the location counter value for *input* is 2000, what is the location counter value for the number 20?

16. Modify the factorial program of Figure 1–2 to calculate the factorial of a number stored in memory location *num*.

17. What is the "." called in the binary fraction 1011.1101?

Chapter 4

VAX Instruction Set and Addressing Modes

4.1 Vax Instruction Set

The designers of the VAX-11 had available to them over two decades of experience and knowledge about computers. In particular, they had become aware of the following truism:

One of the major uses of computers is to run computer programs.

Having made this discovery, it was a short step to discovering what constructs are most frequently used in computer programming. Knuth [8], in a famous paper written in 1971, reports the following about the statements in a typical FORTRAN program:

51% are *assignment* statements.
10% are *if* statements.
 9% are *goto*'s.
 9% are *do*'s.
 5% are *call*'s.

Of the assignment statements, the vast majority are of the form

```
        a=a op 1
or      a=a op n
or      a=a op b
or      a=b op c
```

(*op* is any one of the arithmetic operators +, *, etc.; *n* is any constant; and *a, b,* and *c* represent variables.)

In follow-up papers Alexander et al. [1], Elshoff [4], and Robinson and Torsun [12] report similar results for XPL, PL/I, and later versions of FORTRAN.

The VAX instruction set (called VAX/MACRO) is designed to reflect these studies. Thus there is an instruction to add (or subtract) 1 from an operand:

```
incl a ; a:=a+1
```

where *a* is the symbolic name for a location containing a longword. There are versions of this instruction (*incb, incw,* and *incq*) for bytes, words, and quadwords, respectively.

Similarly, there is a single instruction representing the common assignment statement *a:=a+b:*

```
addl2 b,a ; a:=a+b
```

and for *a:=b+c:*

```
addl3 b,c,a ; a:=b+c
```

Counterparts for these instructions also exist for subtraction, multiplication, and division.

There are branch and jump instructions representing *goto*'s, and single instructions which simulate the loop structure:

```
loop  for index:=m to n
         .
         .
         .
end    loop
```

There are also single instructions for calling subroutines and procedures.

The following sections describe and give examples of the various VAX-11 assembly language instructions. They are divided into the following groups:

Move instructions
Arithmetic instructions
Address manipulation instructions
Compare-and-branch (control) instructions
Miscellaneous instructions

Not all VAX-11 instructions are described in this text. In particular, queue instructions, and packed decimal string instructions are not discussed. For more information concerning these, see Levy and Eckhouse [9] and the *VAX-11 Architecture Handbook* [14].

Move instructions

In high-level languages, values are *assigned* to variables. For example:

```
a:=3
```

assigns the value 3 to the variable *a*. On the machine level this is accomplished by moving (i.e., copying) the integer 3 to the location whose name is *a:*

```
movl #3,a ; a:=3
```

Move

The move instruction has the following format and meaning:

```
mov_ source,destination
```

copies the number of bytes indicated in _ from the address specified by *source* to the address specified by *destination*. The _ (in *mov_*) indicates that this instruction comes in different "flavors." The following table shows the various choices:

Opcode	Mnemonic	Meaning
90	movb	Move byte
B0	movw	Move word
D0	movl	Move long
7D	movq	Move quad
50	movf	Move floating

EXAMPLE

```
56 01 B0 movw #1,r6 ; initialize register 6 to 1
```

The machine code for this instruction is shown to the left of the assembly language code. *Note:* The programmer does not write the machine code (56 01 B0). The assembler translates the instruction *movw #1,r6* into this machine code. We will occasionally show the machine code to the left of the instructions. This is the way the assembly listing (the listing after assembly) shows it.

EXAMPLE

```
57 56 90 movb r6,r7
```

Register 6's rightmost byte is put into the rightmost byte of Register 7. Note that the leftmost three bytes in Register 7 remain the same.

Move negated

```
mneg_ source,destination
```

moves a copy of the *negative* of the *source* to the *destination*.

Opcode	Mnemonic
8E	mnegb
AE	mnegw
CE	mnegl
52	mnegf

EXAMPLE

```
57 01 CE mnegl #1,r7 ; put -1 into register 7
```

EXAMPLE

```
59 58 52 mnegf r8,r9 ; replace register 9 with the
                     ; negative of the contents of
                     ; register 8
```

Thus if Register 8 contains 00004100_{16} (= 2.0_{10}), then after this instruction is executed, Register 9 contains $0000C100_{16}$ (= -2.0_{10}).

Move complemented

```
mcom_ source,destination
```

moves the *source* operand to the *destination* operand, changing all 0's to 1's and 1's to 0's. (This is known as the logical complement.) Thus the logical complement of 11010010 is 00101101.

Opcode	Mnemonic
92	mcomb
B2	mcomw
D2	mcoml

EXAMPLE

```
57 50 D2 mcoml r0,r7
```

If Register 0 contains 00004010_{16}, then Register 7 contains $FFFFBFEF_{16}$ after this instruction is executed. (To see this more clearly, convert both of these quantities to binary.)

Move zero-extended

```
movz_ source,destination
```

moves the (smaller-sized) *source* to the (larger-sized) *destination*, filling the left part of the *destination* with 0's.

Opcode	Mnemonic	Meaning
9B	movzbw	Move zero-extended byte to word
9A	movzbl	Move zero-extended byte to long
3C	movzwl	Move zero-extended word to long

EXAMPLE

```
57 5A 3C movzwl r10,r7
```

If Register 10 contains $1234ABCD_{16}$ and Register 7 contains $EFEF1234_{16}$, then after this instruction is executed, Register 7 contains $0000ABCD_{16}$.

We will use *move zero-extended* rather than *move* when we want to be sure that the more significant bits of a destination are 0.

Clear instructions

```
clr_ destination
```

initializes the destination to 0.

Opcode	Mnemonic	Meaning
94	clrb	Clear byte
B4	clrw	Clear word
D4	clrl	Clear long
D4	clrf	Clear floating
7C	clrq	Clear quad

(Why is there only one machine code for *clrl* and *clrf* ?)

EXAMPLE

```
clrw a
```

clears (fills with 0's) 16 bits starting at address *a*.

EXAMPLE

```
50 7C clrq r0
```

clears both R0 and the next register R1.

Converting from one data type to another

```
cvt_ source,destination
```

moves the *source* to the *destination*, changing its data type. The *source* operand is not affected.

Opcode	Mnemonic	Meaning
99	cvtbw	Convert byte to word
98	cvtbl	Convert byte to long
33	cvtwb	Convert word to byte
32	cvtwl	Convert word to long
F6	cvtlb	Convert long to byte
F7	cvtlw	Convert long to word
4C	cvtbf	Convert byte to float
4D	cvtwf	Convert word to float
4E	cvtlf	Convert long to float
48	cvtfb	Convert float to byte (truncates)
49	cvtfw	Convert float to word (truncates)
4A	cvtfl	Convert float to long (truncates)
4B	cvtrfl	Convert float to long (rounds)

EXAMPLE

```
56 57 49 cvtfw r7,r6
```

If Register 7 contains 00004100_{16} (= 2.0_{10}), then after this instruction is executed, Register 6 contains 00000002_{16} (= 2_{10}).

EXAMPLE

```
56 02 4E cvtlf #2,r6
```

converts the longword integer (= 00000002_{16}) to floating point 2.0_{10} (= 00004100_{16}).

Rotate instructions

```
rotl n,source,destination
```

moves the *source* to the *destination*, rotating it circularly n bits. The rotation is to the left if n is positive and to the right if n is negative.

Opcode	Mnemonic
9C	rotl

EXAMPLE

```
57 56 10 9C rotl #16,r6,r7
```

If Register 6 contains EEEE1234$_{16}$, then after this instruction is executed, Register 7 will contain 1234EEEE$_{16}$.

Rotating to the left one place essentially performs a multiplication by 2, as the reader can check. Similarly, rotating to the right is equivalent to a division by 2.

```
ashl n,source,destination
```

again rotates the source as it is moved to the destination. However, the rotation is not circular. In fact, ash stands for *arithmetic shift*. If the shift is to the left (*n* positive), then 0's are brought in on the right, and if the shift is to the right (*n* negative), then copies of the most significant (i.e., leftmost) bit are brought in from the left.

Opcode	Mnemonic
78	ashl

EXAMPLE

```
57 56 10 78 ashl #16,r6,r7
```

If Register 6 contains EEEE1234$_{16}$, then after this instruction is executed, Register 7 contains 12340000$_{16}$.

Arithmetic instructions

Incrementing by 1

```
inc_ operand
```

adds 1 to the *operand*.

Opcode	Mnemonic
96	incb
B6	incw
D6	incl

EXAMPLE

```
59 D6 incl r9
```

adds 1 to the contents of Register 9.

Decrementing by 1

```
dec_ operand
```

subtracts 1 from the *operand*.

Opcode	Mnemonic
97	decb
B7	decw
D7	decl

EXAMPLE

```
decw a
```

subtracts 1 from the 16 bits whose address is *a*.

Addition

```
add_2 operand1,operand2
```

adds the contents of *operand1* to the contents of *operand2* and the result is stored in *operand2*.

```
add_3 operand1,operand2,operand3
```

adds the contents of *operand1* to the contents of *operand2* and the result is stored in *operand3*.

Opcode	Mnemonic
80	addb2
81	addb3
A0	addw2
A1	addw3
C0	addl2
C1	addl3
40	addf2
41	addf3

EXAMPLE

```
addf2 #2.0,sum
```

If *sum* initially contains 0, then after this instruction is executed, *sum* contains 2.0_{10} (= 00004100_{16}).

EXAMPLE

```
addf3 #2.0,sum1,sum
```

If *sum1* initially contains 00004100_{16} (= 2.0_{10}), then after this instruction is executed, *sum* contains 00004180_{16} (= 4.0_{10}). *Sum1* is not changed.

Subtraction

```
sub_2 operand1,operand2
```

subtracts the contents of *operand1* from *operand2* and stores the result in *operand2*.

```
sub_3 operand1,operand2,operand3
```

subtracts the contents of *operand1* from *operand2* and stores the result in *operand3*.

Opcode	Mnemonic
82	subb2
83	subb3
A2	subw2
A3	subw3
C2	subl2
C3	subl3
42	subf2
43	subf3

EXAMPLE

```
subf2 #2.0,sum
```

If *sum* initially contains 00004180_{16} (= 4.0_{10}), then after this instruction executes, it will contain 00004100_{16} (= 2.0_{10}).

Note the order in which the subtraction is done on the operands.

Multiplication

```
mul_2 operand1,operand2
```

multiplies *operand1* by *operand2* and the result is stored in *operand2*.

```
mul_3 operand1,operand2,operand3
```

multiplies *operand1* by *operand2* and the result is stored in *operand3*.

Opcode	Mnemonic
84	mulb2
85	mulb3
A4	mulw2
A5	mulw3
C4	mull2
C5	mull3
44	mulf2
45	mulf3

EXAMPLE

```
57 58 44 mulf2 r8,r7
```

If Register 8 and Register 7 each initially contain 00004100_{16} ($= 2.0_{10}$), then after this instruction is executed, Register 7 contains 00004180_{16} ($= 4.0_{10}$).

Division

```
div_2 operand1,operand2
```

divides *operand2* by *operand1* and the stores result in *operand2*.

```
div_3 operand1,operand2,operand3
```

divides *operand2* by *operand1* and stores the result in *operand3*.

Opcode	Mnemonic
86	divb2
87	divb3
A6	divw2
A7	divw3
C6	divl2
C7	divl3
46	divf2
47	divf3

EXAMPLE

```
58 57 46 divf2 r7,r8
```

If Register 7 contains 00004100_{16} ($= 2.0_{10}$) and Register 8 contains 00004180_{16} ($= 4.0_{10}$), then after this instruction executes, Register 8 contains 00004100_{16} ($= 2.0_{10}$).

Again, note that the contents of R8 are divided by the contents of R7, not vice versa.

Writing a small program

We will use some of the move and arithmetic instructions to write a small program.

Problem: Write an assembly language program to find the average of two word integers x and y. (Use $x = 2$ and $y = 3$ for data.)

Discussion: We must calculate the following:

$$\text{Average:= } (x + y) / 2$$

Since x and y are stored as (word) integers, we must convert their sum before dividing by 2 (since the answer may not be an integer). The program is shown in Figure 4–1.

Move address instructions

```
mova_ source,destination
```

copies the *address* of the *source* into the *destination*.

Opcode	Mnemonic
9E	movab
3E	movaw
DE	moval
DE	movaf
7E	movaq

EXAMPLE

```
moval table,rl
```

gets the address of table and stores this address in Register 1.

We will use the *move address* instructions frequently when we deal with arrays.

Figure 4–1.

```
x:        .word    2
y:        .word    3
avg:      .float
sum:      .word
begin:    .word
          addw3    x,y,sum     ;sum: = x + y
          cvtwf    sum,avg     ;avg: = sum
          divf2    #2.0,avg    ;avg: = avg / 2
          ret
          .end     begin
```

Compare-and-branch instructions

Compare instructions

```
cmp_ operand1,operand2
```

compares *operand1* with *operand2*. The condition codes in the PSL are set according to the outcome of the comparison:

> Z is set if they are equal; otherwise Z is cleared.
> N is set if operand1 is less than operand2.

Opcode	Mnemonic
91	cmpb
B1	cmpw
D1	cmpl
51	cmpf

The compare instructions set or clear the condition codes. The branch instructions test the condition codes and branch, that is, *goto* based upon the result of the comparison.

```
b_ label
```

branches to *label* based on the contents of the condition codes.
A *cmp* instruction is usually followed by a *branch* instruction.

```
tst_ operand
```

compares the operand with 0. The condition codes are set or cleared as a result of the comparison:

> Z is set if the operand is 0; otherwise it is cleared.
> N is set if the operand is negative; otherwise it is cleared.

A *tst* instruction is also usually followed by a *branch* instruction.

Opcode	Mnemonic
95	tstb
B5	tstw
D5	tstl
53	tstf

Branch instructions

Opcode	Mnemonic	Meaning
12	bneq	Branch if not equal (i.e., if Z = 0)
13	beql	Branch if equal (i.e., if Z = 1)
14	bgtr	Branch if greater (i.e., if Z or N is 0)
15	bleg	Branch if less than or equal to (N or Z is 1)
18	bgeq	Branch if greater than or equal to (N = 0)
19	blss	Branch if less (N = 1)

EXAMPLE

```
cmpl    r0,rl    ; compares r0 with rl
bgtr    there    ; if r0>rl, (i.e., N=0), branch to there
        .
        .
        .
there:
```

Each of these branch instructions has an "unsigned" counterpart which ignores the signs of the operands. Thus,

```
cmpl    r0,rl
bgtru   there
```

would cause a branch to *there* if $|r0| > |r1|$.

Opcode	Mnemonic	Meaning
12	bnequ	Branch if not equal unsigned
13	beqlu	Branch if equal unsigned
1A	bgtru	Branch if greater unsigned
1B	blequ	Branch if less than or equal unsigned
1E	bgequ	Branch if greater than or equal unsigned
1F	blssu	Branch if less unsigned

Also, there are branch instructions which test the condition codes directly.

Opcode	Mnemonic	Meaning
1E	bcc	Branch if carry clear
1F	bcs	Branch if carry set
1C	bvc	Branch if overflow clear
1D	bvs	Branch if overflow set

And finally, there are unconditional branch instructions which branch a certain number of bytes away in the program. To unconditionally branch a larger number of bytes away the instruction *jmp* must be used.

Opcode	Mnemonic	Meaning
11	brb	Branch less than 128 bytes away
31	brw	Branch less than 32768 bytes away

Jump instruction

```
jmp label
```

transfers execution to the instruction at *label:*

Opcode	Mnemonic
17	jmp

EXAMPLE

```
jmp    there   ; unconditional branch to there
       .
       .
       .
there:
```

Another program

We will use some of the instructions from the last two sections as well as some from the previous sections to calculate the absolute value of a number *x*.

Problem: Write an assembly language program to put the absolute value of a word integer *x* into Register 6.

Discussion: The problem requires us to calculate

$$R6 := |x|$$

But since *x* is 16 bits and Register 6 is 32 bits, we must make sure that the most significant 16 bits of Register 6 contain 0. The program is shown in Figure 4–2.

Loop instructions

Counting up by 1's

Most compiler languages have instructions which implement the loop structure:

```
loop for index=m to n
                .
                .
                .
end loop
```

Here, *index* is initialized to *m* and the instructions represented by the three dots are executed. At the end of the loop, *m* is increased by 1, compared to *n*, and if $m \leq n$, the loop is executed again.

This loop structure is implemented in VAX assembly language using *aobleq:*

```
aobleq limit,index,label
```

tells the CPU to add 1 to *index;* if *index* $\leq$ *limit*, go to *label*. There is also an instruction that *adds* *one* and *branches* on *less:*

```
aoblss limit,index,label
```

Opcode	Mnemonic
F3	aobleq
F2	aoblss

EXAMPLE

```
        movl m,index
loop:    .
         .
         .
        aobleq n,index,loop
```

implements the loop structure described previously. Note that *index* is initialized before the loop is entered. The factorial program from Chapter 1 uses *aobleq*. Both the algorithm and the program are repeated in Figure 4–3.

Figure 4–2.

```
x:      .word    -4
;
begin:  .word
        tstw     x      ; if x>0
        bgeq     pos    ;   then go to pos
        mnegw    x,x    ;   else x:=-x
pos:    movzwl   x,r6   ; R6:=x
        ret
        .end     begin
```

Counting down by 1's

The designers of the VAX realized that many loops count *down* rather than *up*. The following loop counts *down:*

```
loop   for index=n down to 1
           .
           .
           .

       end loop
```

Here, *index* is initialized to *n*. The instructions represented by the three dots are executed for *index* = *n*. At the end of the loop, *index* is decremented by 1 and compared with 1. If *index* is greater than or equal to 1 (i.e., greater than 0), then the loop is executed again.

This loop structure is implemented on the VAX with sobgtr:

```
sobgtr index,label
```

tells the CPU to subtract one from *index;* if *index* > 0, branch to *label*. There is also an instruction *sobgeq* which says to subtract *one* and *branch* if *greater than or equal* to 0.

```
sobgeq index,label
```

Opcode	Mnemonic	Meaning
F4	sobgeq	Subtract 1 and branch if ≥ 0
F5	sobgtr	Subtract 1 and branch if > 0

Figure 4–3.

```
; fact:= 1
; loop for i:= 1 to 10 do
;          fact:= fact*i
; end loop
;
fact:      .long
;
begin:     .word
           movl   #1,fact      ;fact:=1
           movl   #1,r6        ;i:=1
loop:      mull2  r6,fact      ;fact:=fact*i
           aobleq #10,r6,loop  ;i:=i+1
           ret
           .end   begin
```

EXAMPLE

```
        movl n,index
  loop: .

        .
        .

        sobgtr index,loop
```

implements the loop described above.

We can compute 10 factorial by counting *down* from 10 as well as by counting *up* to 10. The following algorithm does this:

```
n:=10
loop for i:=9 down to 1
        n:=n*i
end loop
```

The first line initializes *n* to 10. The next line is the first line of a loop which initializes *i* to 9 and subtracts 1 from it each time through the loop. Each time through the loop, *n* is assigned the value $n \times i$. When $i = 1$, the loop is finished. The program is shown in Figure 4–4.

Counting by increments other than 1

The instructions *aobleq*, *aoblss*, *sobgtr*, and *sobgeq* allow us to implement loop structures that count up or down by increments or decrements of 1. Sometimes the programmer may wish to implement a loop structure that counts by, say, 2's or –3's:

Figure 4–4.

```
;   this program calculates 10 factorial (10!)
;   by the method 10*9*8* . . .
;
; fact   :=1
; loop for i:= 10 to 1 do
;         fact:= fact*i
; end loop
;
  fact:     .long
  begin:    .word
            movl    #1,fact     ; fact:=1
            movl    #10,r6      ; i:=10
  loop:     mull2   r6,fact     ; fact:=fact*i
            sobgtr  r6,loop     ; i:=i-1
            ret
            .end    begin
```

```
loop    for index=m to (or down to) n by amount

                         .

                         .

                         .

end     loop
```

Here, *index* is initialized to *m* and the instructions represented by the three dots are executed. At the end of the loop, *m* is increased by *amount* (or decreased if *amount* is negative); if *index* ≤ *n* (or *index* ≥ *n* if *amount* is negative), the loop is executed again.

The following instructions exist for this type of looping:

```
acb  limit,amount,index,label
```

tells the CPU to add *amount* to *index*—replacing the value in *index*. If *amount* > 0 and *index* ≤ *limit*, then branch to *label*. Or if *amount* < 0 and *index* ≥ *limit*, then branch to *label*.

Note that this instruction can be used for both counting up and counting down. If *amount* is positive, then *index* counts *up* to *limit;* if *amount* is negative, then *index* counts *down* to *limit*.

Opcode	Mnemonic	Meaning
9D	acbb	Add, compare (bytes), and branch
3D	acbw	Add, compare (words), and branch
F1	acbl	Add, compare (longs), and branch
4F	acbf	Add, compare (floats), and branch

EXAMPLE

```
        movl m,index
loop:  .

        .

        .

        acbl n,amount,index,loop
```

implements the loop structure described above.

A program

Problem: Write an assembly language program to convert the temperatures between 25.0°F and 26.0°F (by tenths) to Celsius.

Discussion: The following algorithm is easily arrived at:

```
loop for temp:=25.0 to 26.0 by 0.1
        c:=5/9(temp-32.0)
   end loop
```

The assembly language program to implement this is shown in Figure 4–5.

Miscellaneous instructions

These will be introduced as needed; for example, stack instructions are discussed in Chapter 6.

Implementing a mod function

Many computer languages, including FORTRAN, BASIC, and Pascal, include a "mod" function which is used to compute remainders on integer division. Thus *mod(a,b)* computes the *remainder* when the integer *a* is divided by the integer *b*. For example, *mod(5,2)* is 1 and *mod(5,3)* is 2. The mod function is implemented on the VAX with *ediv*:

```
ediv divisor,dividend,quotient,remainder
```

divides the quadword (it must be a quadword) dividend by the longword divisor. The result is stored in the longword quotient and longword remainder, respectively. The following program uses *ediv*.

A program

Problem: Write an assembly language program to test whether an integer *n* is even. If *n* is even, put a 0 into Register 6; otherwise put a 1 into Register 6.

Discussion: We know that even numbers have no remainder when divided by 2. Thus we wish to code the following algorithm.

```
if mod(n,2)=0
   then r6:=0
   else r6:=1
```

Figure 4–5.

```
        frac = ^F5/9
temp:   .float
begin:  .word
        movf    #25.0,temp          ;temp:= 25.0
loop:   subf3   #32.0,temp,r6       ;c:= temp - 32.0
        mulf2   #frac,r6            ;c:= c * 5 /9
        acbf    #26.0,#0.1,temp,loop ;temp:= temp + 0.1
        ret
        .end    begin
```

The program is shown in Figure 4–6.

There are other instructions for performing extended arithmetic operations:

```
emul
```

instructs the CPU to perform extended multiply.

```
adwc   and   sbwc
```

are used for carrying in addition and borrowing in subtraction, respectively. In addition,

```
xor_
```

performs the exclusive-or operation. We refer the interested reader to the VAX architecture handbook [14] for details on these instructions.

Another miscellaneous instruction and an appropriate one with which to end this section is

```
ret
```

which means to transfer control from a procedure back to a calling procedure. This instruction is also used in main programs to transfer control back to the operating system. Frequently, the instruction

```
movl #1,r0   or   movzbl #1,r0
```

is included before *ret* to indicate successful completion of the program.

4.2 Addressing Modes

VAX-11 instructions specify addresses of data in various ways. Sometimes the operand is itself the address:

Figure 4–6.

```
; This program takes an integer n, and calculates
; n mod 2.
;
  n:        .quad   9               ; n:=9
;
  begin:    .word
            ediv    #2,n,r5,r6   ; r6:= n mod 2
            ret
            .end    begin
```

EXAMPLE

```
movl r0,store
```

Here, both R0 and *store* are the actual addresses of the data. The CPU goes to R0 and copies the contents into the memory location whose name is *store*.

It is sometimes the case that the operand contains the *address* of the data rather than the actual data.

EXAMPLE

```
movl (r0),store
```

Here the parentheses mean that R0 contains the *address* of the data. The CPU goes to that address (called the *effective address*) and copies those contents into memory location *store*. This is an example of *indirect addressing*.

Similarly *store* may not be the location we wish to copy into. Possibly *store* contains the address of the location to be copied into:

EXAMPLE

```
movl r0,@store
```

Here the contents of Register 0 are copied not to location *store* but to the location specified in *store*. (Clearly, an address had to, in some way, be put into *store* before this instruction is executed.)

Note that () is used for indirect referencing of registers and @ is used for indirect referencing of memory locations.

When the operand of an instruction involves a register, this address specification is called an addressing mode. We will discuss each of these separately.

Each addressing mode has its own machine code called a mode specifier. This mode specifier occupies a half-byte (called a nibble!) of the machine language code. Following are descriptions of most of the basic addressing modes.

Register mode

We use register mode (mode specifier = 5) when the register contains the actual contents to be operated upon. This is the simplest of the addressing modes and is sometimes called *direct addressing*. All the examples in this text so far have used registers in register mode—that is, all the registers have contained the actual contents to be operated on.

EXAMPLE

```
57 56 D0 movl r6,r7
```

As in Section 4.1, the machine code is shown to the left of the instruction as it would appear after assembly. D0 is the opcode for *movl*, and 56 denotes register mode (the 5) on register 6 (the 6). Similarly, 57 denotes that Register 7 is used in register mode. If Register 6 contains $00A03412_{16}$, then after this instruction is executed, Register 7 will also contain $00A03412_{16}$—regardless of its initial contents.

Register deferred mode

We use register deferred mode (mode specifier = 6) when the register contains the *address* of the data rather than the actual data. It is denoted by enclosing the register in parentheses (Rn), where n is any of the integers from 0 to 15.

EXAMPLE

Machine code				Location	Assembly language		
00000006 0000000A 00000004 0000000F				0000	list:	.long	15,4,10,6,4
			00000004	0010			
			0000	0014	start:	.word	
	56	E7AF	DE	0016		moval	list,r6
	55	66	D0	001A		movl	(r6), r5
				001D		.end	start

After *movl (r6),r5* is executed, Register 5 will contain $0000000F_{16}$ (= 15_{10}). Note that the location counter value is printed out in this example. The actual assembly listing would also print this out.

Autoincrement mode

We use autoincrement mode (mode specifier = 8) to step automatically through consecutive locations such as arrays. Once again, the register is assumed to contain the *address* of the data. After this instruction is executed, however, this address is updated to contain the next address. Autoincrement mode is denoted by enclosing the register in parentheses and following it with a "+", that is, (Rn)+.

EXAMPLE

Machine code				Location	Assembly language		
00000006 0000000A 00000004			0000000F	0000	list:	.long	15,4,10,6,4
			00000004	0010			
			0000	0014	start:	.word	
	56	E7 AF	DE	0016		moval	list,r6
	55	86	D0	001A		movl	(r6)+,r5
				001D		.end	start

After *movl (r6)+,r5* is executed, Register 5 contains the 15. Register 6 is updated (by a longword since that is what was moved) so that it contains the address of the 4. Thus (r6) contains 00000004_{16} since the second element of list, the 4, is at location 0004.

We will use the previous three addressing modes in the program that follows.

Looking for blanks

Problem: Write a program which counts the number of blanks in a short line of text. Use the following as data:

```
text: .ascii / b l an k s /
```

Put the number of blanks into Register 6.

Discussion: text is a list of byte-sized values starting at address *text*. Each ASCII character is stored in a byte. Thus if we move this address to a register, we can use autoincrement to step through *text* byte by byte. We can use the following method to compute (at assembly time—see Chapter 3) the length of this text:

```
text: .ascii / b l an k s /
      length = .-text
```

The complete program is shown in Figure 4–7.

Autodecrement mode

We use autodecrement mode (mode specifier = 7) for stepping through consecutive locations in reverse. Thus, once again, the register contains the *address* of the data rather than the actual data. However, this address is decreased to the previous datum *before* the instruction is executed. Autodecrement is denoted by preceding the parentheses with a "–", that is, –(R*n*).

Machine code				Location	Assembly language		
00000006	0000000A	00000004	0000000F	0000	list:	.long	15,4,10,6,4
			00000004	0010			
			0000	0014	start:	.word	
	56	FB AF	3E	0016		movaw	start,r6
	55	76	D0	001A		movl	–(r6),r5
				001D		.end	start

After *movl –(r6),r5* is executed, Register 5 will contain the last element in *list*, the 4.

Reversing a list

Problem: Write an assembly language program to reverse the elements in a list. Use the following as data:

```
input: .ascii /abcdefghijklmn/
```

Store the reversed list at location *output*.

Figure 4–7.
```
text:     .ascii  /b l an k s /
          length = .-text
          blank  = ^A/ /
index:    .long
;
begin:    .word
          clrl    r6                    ; r6:= 0
          moval   text,r7               ; r7 contains address text
          clrl    index                 ; index:= 0
loop:     cmpb    #blank,(r7)+          ; if contents of location whose
          bneq    contin                ; address is in R7 is a blank
          incl    r6                    ;    then R6:= R6 + 1
contin:   aoblss  #length,index,loop    ; index:= index +1
          ret
          .end    begin
```

Discussion: We can use autoincrement to move forward from the beginning of our input list and autodecrement to store backward from the end of our output list:

Input	Output
a	n
b	m
.	.
. .	.
.	.
m	b
n	a

We will need to calculate *length,* the number of elements; we will also need to allot *length* bytes for *output;* and we will need to store the addresses of *input* and *output+length* into separate registers. The program is shown in Figure 4–8.

Autoincrement deferred

We use autoincrement deferred (mode specifier = 9) to access a list of addresses (of elements) rather than a list of elements. Thus the register contains the *address* of an *address* rather than the *address* of an *element*! Although this seems somewhat complicated, programmers find this mode useful when it is convenient or necessary to deal with tables of addresses rather than tables of values. Autoincrement deferred is denoted by @(R*n*)+.

Figure 4–8.

```
input:    .ascii  /abcdefghijklmn/
          length = .-input
output:   .blkb   length
;
begin:    .word
          movab   input,r6    ; R6:= address of input string
          movab   output,r7   ; R7:= address of output string
          movab   begin,r8    ; R8:= R7 + length
loop:     movb    (r6)+.-(r8) ; decrement R8
                              ; move 1 char from input to output
                              ; increment R6
          cmpl    r6,r7       ; compare R6 to address of output string
          bneq    loop        ; if less than or equal, go to loop
          ret
          .end    begin
```

EXAMPLE

Machine code	Location	Assembly language

	00000002	0000	a:	.long	2
	00000003	0004	b:	.long	3
	00000004	0008	c:	.long	4
	00000005	000C	d:	.long	5
	00000006	0010	e:	.long	6
0000000C'00000008'00000004'00000000'	0014	list:	.address	a,b,c,d,e
	00000010'	0024			
	0000	0028	start:	.word	
56 E7 AF DE	002A		moval	list,r6
55 96 D0	002E		movl	@(r6)+,r5
	0031		.end	start

After *movl @(r6)+,r5* is executed, Register 5 contains a 2 and Register 6 contains the address of the next item in *list* (which is itself the address b).

Displacement mode

We use byte displacement mode (mode specifier = A) to access data which occurs at a byte displacement from the address in our register. The (integer) displacement precedes the ()'s. Thus *2(r7)* refers to an item 2 bytes beyond the address in Register 7. *2(r7)* may also be written *b^2(r7)*, where the "b" refers to byte.

EXAMPLE

Machine code	Location	Assembly language

0000000A 00000006 00000004 0000000F	0000	list:	.long	15,4,6,10,4
	00000004	0010			
	0000	0014	start:	.word	
58 E7 AF DE	0016		moval	list,r8
04 A8 68 D1	001A		cmpl	(r8),4(r8)
	001E		.end	start

The instruction *cmpl (r8),4(r8)* compares the 15 with the 4. Note that the machine code for *4(r8)* is 04 A8. That is, the machine code for byte deferred Register 8 (A8) is followed (reading right to left) by the actual number of bytes displaced (04).

Displacement deferred

We use displacement deferred mode (mode specifier = B) to access offsets when the datum is an address. Thus we assume that the register contains the address of an address and we wish to access the data at a displacement. Displacement deferred is denoted by preceding the m (Rn) with @, that is, @m(Rn) where m is the actual displacement.

EXAMPLE

```
list1:   .long      15,4,6,10,4
list2:   .long      4,6,10,15,4
list3:   .long      10,4,6,4,15
table:   .address   list1,list2,list3
start:   .word
         moval      table,r6
         movl       @8(r6),r5
         .end       start
```

After *movl @8(r6),r5* is executed, Register 5 contains a 10 since *table +8* contains the address of *list3;* that is, *8(r6)* contains the address of *list3.* Then *@8(r6)* contains 10—the first item in *list3.*

Literal mode and immediate mode

We have already seen these modes. They are used for dealing with constants (or expressions). Literal mode is used for short constants—for example, the integers between 0 and 63. Immediate mode is used for longer constants. The assembler decides which mode to use. For example,

```
movl #2,r6
```

We say that the #2 is in literal mode.

Other modes

There are other addressing modes which we haven't discussed here—for example, absolute mode and general mode. The *VAX-11 MACRO Language Reference Manual* [17] contains a description of all the available addressing modes.

Index registers

Addressing modes enable the programmer to access the base address of a table (or array) of data. Index registers are used to access particular elements in the array—that is, to compute the index or subscript. Index mode is denoted by [Rx], where x stands for one of the registers between 0 and 12. The mode specifier for index registers is 4. Thus

```
(r6)[r7]
```

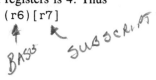

indicates that Register 6 contains the base (beginning) address of an array and we wish to access the element whose index (subscript) is in Register 7.

In assembly language, we usually consider arrays as subscripted from 0. That is, we consider a_0, a_1, a_2, . . . rather than a_1, a_2, a_3, ... Thus

> (r6) [r7]

refers to a_4 if Register 6 contains the address of a_0 and Register 7 contains a 4. More formally, we perform the following steps to evaluate

> (Rn) [Rx]

Step 1: Compute the base address contained in Rn.

Step 2: Take the value stored in the index register Rx and multiply it by the size in bytes implied by the operation.

Step 3: Add the value calculated in step 2 to the address calculated in step 1. This is the effective address.

The contents of the index register are not changed. Other addressing modes may be used with index registers as well as register deferred. Only register mode is not allowed.

EXAMPLE

Machine code				Location	Assembly language		
0000000A	00000006	00000004	0000000F	0000	list:	.long	15,4,6,10,4
			00000004	0010			
			0000	0014	start:	.word	
		58	E7 AF DE	0016		moval	list,r8
		59	02 9A	001A		movzbl	#2,r9
		5A 6849	D0	001D		movl	(r8)[r9],r10
				0021		.end	start

After execution of *movl (r8)[r9],r10*, Register 10 will contain *list$_2$*, which is 6. (Remember that the first element in *list* is *list$_0$*.) We will study arrays and hence index registers in Chapter 5.

4.3 Machine Code Revisited

The machine code for the assembled version of the program from Chapter 1 which calculates $a*b+c$ is repeated in Figure 4–9.

The machine code for the various references to R6 is 56 since R6 is always used in register mode and 5 is the mode specifier for register mode.

It is now possible to understand the machine code for the various references to *a*,*b*, *c*, and *result*. We must remind ourselves of four facts:

1. During execution Register 15 contains the address of the *next* operand or instruction.
2. $15_{10} = F_{16}$.
3. Displacements may be negative in displacement mode.
4. Negative numbers are stored using two's complement.

Consider the machine code for *movl a,r6*:

```
56 EB AF D0 0012 movl a,r6
```

Although this program is relocated at link time, the relative locations remain the same. We will thus deal with the locations as though they were actual *(absolute)*. Chapter 12 discusses this concept further.

The AF is byte displacement mode on Register 15 since A is the mode specifier for byte displacement and F stands for Register 15. At the time that EB is being processed, Register 15, the program counter contains the address of the next byte, the location of 56. This is location 0015, since D0 is in location 0012_{16}:

```
56      EB      AF      D0      0012 movl a,r6

↑       ↑       ↑       ↑
0015    0014    0013    0012
```

Thus EB indicates the displacement from 0015 to where *a* is stored. But EB is hex for –21 and 0015 = 21. Thus *a* is found to be –21 from the program counter value 21. That is, *a* is in location 0. The arithmetic of machine code is tricky and only practice will make perfect (or even just competent!). We urge the reader to try to verify the machine code for the references to *b*, *c*, and *result* in this program, as well as the machine code for the other examples in this chapter.

Figure 4–9.

		00000002	0000	100 a:		.long	2
		00000003	0004	200 b:		.long	3
		00000004	0008	300 c:		.long	4
		00000000	000C	400 result:		.long	
			0000	0010	500 start:	.word	
56	EB AF	D0	0012	600		movl	a,r6
56	EB AF	C4	0016	700		mull2	b,r6
EC AF 56	EB AF	C1	001A	800		addl3	c,r6,result
		04	0020	900 last:		ret	
			0021	1000		.end	start

Exercises

1. Code the following algorithm into VAX assembly language:

```
loop for   n:=1 to 100 by 2
          nb:=nb+1
          j:=j−1
      endloop
```

2. Write an assembly language program to calculate a^b. Store the result in c.

3. Write a program that calculates $\log(\text{round}(\text{abs}(x)))$ by successive multiplications if $|x| < 1$, and by successive divisions if $|x| \geq 1$.

4. What is a mode specifier? How much space is needed to store one?

5. What addressing modes are particularly useful for stepping through an array?

6. What will be the contents of r6 after the following instruction is executed if the initial contents of r6 is 01011000?

```
movl @(r6)+,r7
```

7. What does the word *deferred* mean in "deferred addressing modes"?

8. Show R2, R4, and *memory* after the following instruction is executed:

```
movl (r2)+,r4
```

The initial values are:

R2 = 00002012
R4 = 00000000
location 00002012 contains 45
location 00002013 contains 67
location 00002014 contains 01
location 00002015 contains 23

9. Write an instruction to move the contents of r6 to the address contained in r7.

Chapter 5

Common Programming Constructs in Assembly Language

5.1 Introduction

In Chapter 1 we saw that a single assignment statement such as

```
result:=a*b+c
```

frequently requires more than one assembly language instruction:

```
mul2 a,b
add3 b,c,result
```

(Although, it is usually faster to move data into registers to perform arithmetic operations, it can also be done from memory locations.) Assignment statements are the most frequently used statements in high-level languages such as BASIC, FORTRAN, and Pascal. Other necessary and common constructs are control statements represented in many languages by *goto*'s, *if*'s, and *if-then-else*'s, and loops represented by *for* loops (*do* loops in FORTRAN), *while* loops, and *repeat* loops. Even though a language may not explicitly contain a construct such as, say, "doing something repeatedly" *while* "some condition is true," the idea is frequently still there implicitly.

In addition, there are certain techniques that a programmer must be familiar with in any language; these include counting, comparing, and dealing with arrays.

The rest of this section features examples of these constructs and techniques. Each will be shown in three forms:

1. Algorithmic form (pseudo-code). In many cases, this is the same as the Pascal.
2. BASIC, FORTRAN (older versions), and Pascal.
3. VAX assembly language.

We hope the reader will become somewhat comfortable in writing his or her own algorithms and in translating from algorithms to assembly language. We chose BASIC, FORTRAN, and Pascal as "intermediaries" because many people are familiar with at least one of them. In the rest of this book, however, only the algorithmic form will be shown before translating to assembly language. (Flow-charts are also a useful way to visualize assembly language logic.)

5.2 Assignment Statements

1. result:= (a+b)*c		
FORTRAN[1]	BASIC	Pascal
result = (a+b)*c	r = (a+b)*c	result:=(a+b)*c
VAX assembly language		

```
            add13   a,b,r6          ; R6:=a+b
            mul13   c,r6,result     ; result:=c*R6
```

2. b:=a²		
FORTRAN	BASIC	Pascal
b=a**2	b=a**2	b:=a*a
VAX assembly language		

```
            mul13      a,a,b     ; b:=a**2
```

3. answer:=((10+save)/(save−8))*4		
FORTRAN	BASIC	Pascal
answer=(10+save)/(save−8)*4	a = (10+s)/(s−8)*4	Same as above
VAX assembly language		

```
            add13   #10,save,r6     ; R6:=save+10
            sub13   #8,save,r5      ; R5:=save−8
            div12   r5,r6           ; R6:=R6/R5
            mul13   r6,#4,result    ; result:=R6*4
```

[1]We presume throughout this section that variable names in FORTRAN and Pascal have been declared to be of the proper type (real or integer.)

5.3 Control (Selection) Statements

If–then and *if-then-else* do not always translate to VAX assembly language easily.

1. if new>max
then max:=new

FORTRAN	BASIC	Pascal
if(new .gt. max)max=new	10 if n>m then 30	if new>max
	20 go to 40	then max:=new
	30 m=n	
	40	

VAX assembly language
cmpl   new,max   ; if new>max
bleq   there
movl   new,max   ; then max:=new
there:

Note that we essentially changed the logic of the program to

```
if new<max
    then
    else max:=new
```

We encourage the reader to try to code this *if–then* statement for him- or herself to try to improve the code.

2. if a<b
then max:=b
else max:=a

FORTRAN[2]	BASIC	Pascal
if(a .lt. b)goto 2	10 if a<b then 40	if a<b
max=a	20 let m=a	then max:=b
go to 3	30 go to 50	else max:=a
2 max=b	40 let m=b	
3	50	

VAX assembly language
cmpl a,b   ; if a<b then
blss lab2 ; go to lab2
movl a,max ; else max:=a
brb lab3   ;
lab2: movl b,max ; max:=b
lab3:

[2] This is "old" FORTRAN. Most newer FORTRAN compilers have implemented the *if-then-else* structure.

Once again, this does not seem to be a "comfortable" translation of the *if-then-else*. We again invite the reader to try to code this better.

5.4 Loops

<table>
<tr><td colspan="3">

```
                  1. sum:=0
                     loop for i:=1 to n
                          sum:=sum+i
                     end  loop
```

</td></tr>
<tr>
<td align="center">FORTRAN</td>
<td align="center">BASIC</td>
<td align="center">Pascal</td>
</tr>
<tr>
<td>

```
sum=0
do 25 i=1,n
   sum=sum+i
25 continue
```

</td>
<td>

```
10 let s=0
20 for i=1 to n
30 let s=s+i
40 next i
```

</td>
<td>

```
sum:=0;
for i:=1 to n do
   sum:=sum+i
```

</td>
</tr>
<tr><td colspan="3">

VAX assembly language

Version 1: Using register mode
```
             clrl    sum       ; sum:=0
             movl    #1,r5     ; r5:=1
     loop:   addl2   r5,sum    ; sum:=sum+r5
             aobleq  n,r5,loop
```
Version 2: Using register deferred mode
```
             clrl    sum
             moval   sum,r4
             movl    #1,r5
     loop:   addl2   r5,(r4)
             aobleq  #n,r5,loop
```

</td></tr>
</table>

(Version 2 is not "better" than version 1; we give it as an example using register deferred mode.)

```
                              2. sum:=0
                                 i:=0
                                 loop while sum≤1000
                                         i:=i+1
                                         sum:=sum+i
                                 end  loop
```

FORTRAN	BASIC	Pascal
sum=0	10 s=0	sum:=0;
do 25 i=1,1000	20 for i=1 to 1000	i:=0;
if(sum.gt.1000)go to 26	30 if s>1000 then 60	while sum<=1000 do
sum=sum+i	40 s=s+1	begin
25 continue	50 next i	i:=i+1;
26	60	sum:=sum+i
		end

VAX assembly language

Version 1: Trying to implement *while* directly

```
                clrl     sum              ; sum:=0
                clrl     r5               ; i:=0
        loop:   cmpl     sum,#1000        ; while sum<=1000
                bgtr     after
                incl     r5               ; i:=i+1
                addl2    r5,sum           ; sum=sum+i
                brb      loop
        after:
```

Version 2: Using aobleq

```
                clrl     sum              ; sum:=0
                movl     #1,r5            ; i:=1
        loop:   cmpl     sum,#1000        ; while sum<=1000
                bgtr     after
                addl2    r5,sum           ; sum=sum+i
                aobleq   #1000,r5,loop    ; i:= i + 1
        after:
```

Notice that it is difficult to code a *while* loop directly. The code is much shorter and easier to read if it is coded as a *for* loop. Version 2 is essentially recoded as a *for* loop.

5.5   Arrays

In Chapter 4 we discussed how to use indexing mode to access array elements. In this section we will illustrate some standard practical problems using arrays.

Finding the largest element in a list

Consider the problem of finding the largest integer in an array *list* of positive integers. Algorithm 1 assumes that the list contains a 0 as the last element.

```
                    1.  i:=1
                      max:=0
                            loop while list_i≠0
                              if list_i>max
                                then max:=list_i
                              end if
                            i:=i+1
                            end loop
```

FORTRAN	BASIC	Pascal

```
max=0                        10 m=0                i:=1;
do 25 i=1,10000              20 for i=1 to 10000   max:=0;
if(list(i).eq.0)goto 26      30 if l(i)=0 then 80  while list [i]<>0 do
if(list(i).gt.max)max=list(i) 40 if l(i)>m then 60   begin
25 continue                  50 go to 70             if list [i]>max
26                           60 m=l(i)                 then max:=list[i];
                             70 next i                i:=i+1
                             80                      end
```

VAX assembly language

```
      start:    .word
                clrw      max
                movaw     list,r7
                tstw      (r7)           ; while list(i)<>0
      loop:     beql      fini
                cmpw      (r7),max       ; if list (i)>max
                bleq      next
                movw      (r7),max       ;   then max:=list(i)
      next:     tstw      (r7)+          ;   i:=i+1
                jmp       loop
      fini:     ret
                .end      start
```

The complete program is shown in Figure 5-1 for the list 102, 5, 1, 412, 999, 0.

Searching

Searching and sorting are two common procedures performed on arrays. We use a search algorithm called a sequential linear search which searches an array sequentially counting the number of occurrences of an item called *key*.

2.	count:=0 loop for i:=1 to n if a$_i$=key then count:=count+1 end if end loop

FORTRAN	BASIC	Pascal
count=0 do 25 i=1,n if(a(i).eq.key)count=count+1 25 continue	10 c=0 20 for i=1 to n 30 if a(i)=k then 50 40 go to 60 50 c=c+1 60 next i	count:=0; for i:=1 to n if a[i]=key then count:=count+1

VAX assembly language

```
        moval    a,r6
        clrl     count
        movzbl   #1,r5
loop:   cmpl     (r6)+,key
        bneq     after
        incl     count
after:  aobleq   #n,r5,loop
```

Figure 5–1.

```
list:   .word   102,5,1,412,999,0
max:    .word
start:  .word
        movaw   list,r7
        tstw    (r7)            ; while list(i)<>0
loop:   beql    fini
        cmpw    (r7),max        ; if list(i) > max
        bleq    next
        movw    (r7),max        ;    then max:= list(i)
next:   tstw    (r7)+           ; i:= i + i
        jmp     loop
fini:   ret
        .end    start
```

The complete program is shown in Figure 5-2. It searches the array *list* counting the number of 3's.

Sorting

The sorting algorithm we describe here is called a selection sort. We shall use this method of sorting to put a list into ascending order. First, we search the list for the smallest element. This is similar to the previous algorithm which searches for the largest element. When we have this smallest element, we then swap it with the first element. Then we search the rest of the list (starting with the second element) looking for the smallest. When we find this (second) smallest element, we swap it with the second element. We continue this procedure next time starting with the third element, then with the fourth, and so on. The procedure is shown below for the list 5, 4, 3, 1, 2:

Pass 1	5	4	3	1	2
Pass 2	1	4	3	5	2
Pass 3	1	2	3	5	4
Pass 4	1	2	3	5	4
Pass 5	1	2	3	4	5

The algorithm on page 87 sorts an array a of n elements using a selection sort (note that the assembly language version is written for the array $a_0, a_1, \ldots, a_{n-1}$ while the algorithm and high-level language versions use array $a_1, a_2, \ldots, a_n$):

Figure 5–2.

```
a:         .long   3,9,41,66,3
           n = <.-a>/4
key:       .long   3
count:     .long
start:     word
           moval   a,r6
           clrl    count              ; count:=0
           movzbl  #1,r5              ; loop for i:= 1 to n
loop:      cmpl    (r6)+,key         ;   if a(i) = key
           bneq    after
           incl    count              ;      then count:= count + 1
after:     aobleq  #n,r5,loop        ; end loop
           ret
           .end    start
```

```
3. loop for i:=1 to n−1
         min:=aᵢ
         place:=i
         loop for j:=i+1 to n
              if aⱼ<min then
                   place:=j
                   min:=aⱼ
              end if
         end   loop
         temp:=aᵢ
         aᵢ:=a_place
         a_place:=temp
   end loop
```

FORTRAN	BASIC	Pascal

```
do 25 i=1,n−1            10 for i=1 to n−1        for i:=1 to n−1 do
   min=a(i)             20 m=a(i)               begin
   place=i              30 p=i                   min:=a[i];
   do 24 j=i+1,n        40 for j=i+1 to n        place:=i;
      if(a(j).ge.min)go to 24   50 if(a(j))<m then 65   for j:=i+1 to n do
      place=j           60 go to 70               if a[j]<min then
      min=a(j)          65 p=j                     begin
24 continue             67 m=a(j)                     place:=j;
   temp=a(i)            70 next j                      min:=a[j]
   a(i)=a(place)        80 t=a(i)                  end
   a(place)=temp        90 a(i)=a(p)            temp:=a[i];
25 continue             100 a(p)=t              a[i]:=a[place];
                        110 next i              a[place]:=temp
                        120                     end
```

VAX assembly language

```
        moval   a,r6
        clrl    r7
loop1:  movl    (r6)[r7],min
        movl    r7,r10
        movl    r7,r9
        incl    r9
loop2:  cmpl    (r6)[r9],min
        bgeq    after
        movl    r9,r10
        movl    (r6)[r9],min
after:  aoblss  #n,r9,loop2
        movl    (r6)[r7],temp
        movl    (r6)[r10],(r6)[r7]
        movl    temp,(r6)[r10]
        aoblss  #n−1,r7,loop1
```

```
a:       .long   5,4,3,1,2
         n = <.-a>/4
min:     .long
temp:    .long
;
start:   .word
         moval   a,r6
         clrl    r7
loop1:   movl    (r6)[r7],min
         movl    r7,r10
         movl    r7,r9
         incl    r9
loop2:   cmpl    (r6)[r9],min
         bgeq    after
         movl    r9,r10
         movl    (r6)[r9],min
after:   aoblss  #n,r9,loop2
         movl    (r6)[r7],temp
         movl    (r6)[r10],(r6)[r7]
         movl    temp,(r6)[r10]
         aoblss  #n-1,r7,loop1
         ret
         .end    start
```

Figure 5–3.

(We encourage the reader to insert the algorithm as comments into the assembly language code.) The complete program is shown in Figure 5-3 for the array consisting of 5, 4, 3, 1, 2.

In this chapter, we have shown how many of the common programming constructs may be implemented in assembly language. Many of these constructs (e.g., *assignment* statements and *for* loops) code easily into VAX assembly language. Others (e.g., *if-then* statements and *while* loops) do not. Programming is not a spectator sport. To become competent at assembly language programming we must practice!

Exercises

1. In the program (Figure 5-1) that finds the maximum element in a list, what is the machine code translation of the following instruction?

   ```
   jmp   loop
   ```

2. Find at least two other ways (from that shown in the text) to code:

   ```
   a. if new > max
         then max:=new
   ```

```
b. if a < b
      then max:=a
      else max:=b
```

3. The following algorithm represents another way of sorting called a bubble sort. Add your own data declarations, code the algorithm into VAX assembly language, and run it.

```
loop for i:=1 to n–1
      loop for j:=1 to n–i
            if aⱼ > aᵢ
                  then temp:=aⱼ
                        aⱼ:=aⱼ₊₁
                        aⱼ₊₁:=temp
            end if
      end loop
end loop
```

[handwritten: BUBBLE SORT =]

4. In Figure 5-3, why was it necessary to compute $n=<.-a>/4$?

5. Write an assembly language program to search through a list and store the address of the first occurrence of a key in a location called *loc*.

[handwritten: IF A(J) > A(I+1)]

Chapter 6

Macros

6.1 Introduction

The VAX instruction set is extensive. We can code in VAX assembly language any algorithm that we can code in a high-level language. There are times, however, when a sequence of the same operations is coded so frequently that we may wish there were a single instruction to perform that sequence of operations. For example, suppose we are writing a program that uses the absolute value of a longword argument in many places. We may find ourselves wishing we could say:

```
        absl      r0        ;           r0:=|r0|
```

or

```
        absl       a        ;           a:=|a|
```

But since there is no such instruction, we code:

```
              tstl       r0
              bgeq       pos
              mnegl      r0,r0
       pos:
```

or

```
              tstl       a
              bgeq       pos
              mnegl      a,a
       pos:
```

each time we want to take an absolute value of some longword argument.

6.2   Defining and Using Macros

Defining a macro

There is, however, a facility in assembly language which allows the programmer to write his or her own instructions. This facility is called a *macro*. Macros are used in assembly language to replace frequently used sequences of code with one instruction. The following defines a macro called *absl*:

```
        .macro        absl x,?pos
          tstl          x
          bgeq          pos
          mnegl         x,x
   pos:   .endm         absl
```

"?" is used in front of any symbol names to be used as labels.

Using a macro

To call the macro in a program, use:

```
   absl          r0        ;    replaces r0 with its
                           ;    absolute value
```

or

```
   absl          a         ;    replaces a with its
                           ;    absolute value
```

The difference between macros and procedures

It may seem that macros are the same as procedures (subroutines). Certainly they are defined once and used many times, as are procedures. However, the assembler implements them differently. During assembly, the assembler replaces each macro call with its definition; this is called *expanding* the macro. Thus, the expansion of:

```
        absl              r0
```

is

```
        tstl              r0
        bgeq              30000$
        mnegl             r0,r0
   30000$:
```

Note that the label has been replaced by a local label. Each time the macro is expanded, a different local label will be generated.

Why use a macro?

Macros do not save storage space. They do, however, save "programmer space"; that is, they allow the programmer to write fewer lines of code. In addition, macros can make assembly language programs more readable by replacing mysterious sequences of code with a mnemonic name—for example, *absl*.

Formal definition

The format for a VAX assembly language macro definition is:

```
.macro    macro-name   formal parameter list
    (body of macro)
.endm     macro-name
```

The formal parameter list may contain labels. Preceding a label by a "?" will ensure that a different local label is generated each time the macro is invoked. Default values may be assigned to the parameters in the formal parameter list (see Chapter 11 and the *VAX-11 MACRO Language Reference Manual* [18]).

Formal call format

The format to call (i.e., use) a macro is

```
macro-name    actual parameter list
```

It is more readable and less error-prone to place all macro definitions prior to the main program.

Using a macro to calculate a∗b+c

We can write a macro that calculates $a*b+c$ and then call it from our main program:

```
.macro    calc  a,b,c,result
    mull3    a,b,r6
    addl3    r6,c,result
.endm     calc
```

An entire program using this macro is shown in Figure 6–1.

Sorting

In the sorting program of Chapter 5, we swap a_{place} with a_i. The program becomes easier to follow with a *swap* macro:

Figure 6–1.

```
.macro  calc    a,b,c,result
  mull3 a,b,r6
  addl3 r6,c,result
.endm   calc
;
start:  .word
        calc    #2,#3,#4,r7
        ret
        .end    start
```

```
                    .macro    swap    x,y     ;  swaps longwords x and y
                      movl    x,temp
                      movl    y,x
                      movl    temp,y
                    .endm     swap
          start:    .word
                       .
                       .
                       .
          after:    aoblss    #n,r9,loop2
                    swap      (r6)[r7],(r6)[r10]
                    aoblss    #n-1,r7,loop1
```

Even though the assembler does replace each macro call with its expansion, this expansion does not occur in the listing unless the following assembler directive is included:

```
  .show   me   ;   show macro expansion
```

Figure 6–2 shows the assembled version of this program (with the *.show me* directive added) for the same array as in Figure 5–3.

Searching

We will implement the search-and-count operation from Figure 5–2 as a macro.

```
.macro    srchcnt    a,n,key,count,?loop,?after
  moval            a,r6
  clrl             count
  movzbl           #1,r5
loop:   cmpl       (r6)+,key
  bneq             after
  incl             count
after:  aobleq     n,r5,loop
  .endm            srchcnt
           .
           .
           .
start:  .word
        srchcnt array,#5,#3,answer   ; put the number of 3's
                                     ; contained in array of 5
                                     ; elements into location answer
           .
           .
           .
```

Figure 6–3 shows the assembled version of this program using the same data as Figure 5–2.

Data initialization

Macros are frequently used to allocate or initialize data. The following initializes an amount *number* of long words to zero starting at location *place:*

```
        .macro    alloc    number,place
        brb       around
place:  .blkl     number
around: .endm   alloc
```

One use of this macro might be to allocate space for $array_0$, $array_1$, $array_2$, . . . , $array_{n-1}$:

```
alloc   100,array
```

Figure 6–2.

```
00000001 00000003 00000004 00000005 0000   1 a:       .long     5,4,3,1,2
                            00000002 0010
                            00000005 0014   2          n = <.-a>/4
                            00000000 0014   3 min:     .long
                            00000000 0018   4 temp:    .long
                                     001C   5
                                     001C   6          .macro    swap x,y
                                     001C   7             movl    x,temp
                                     001C   8             movl    y,x
                                     001C   9             movl    temp, y
                                     001C  10          .endm   swap
                                     001C  11
                                     001C  12          .show    me
                                     001C  13
                             0000    001C  14 start:   .word
            56   DF   AF DE  001E  15           moval    a,r6
                     57   D4 0022  16           clrl     r7
        EB AF     6647   D0 0024  17 loop1:   movl     (r6)[r7],min
            5A     57   D0 0029  18           movl     r7,r10
            59     57   D0 002C  19           movl     r7,r9
                   59   D6 002F  20           incl     r9
        DE AF   6649   D1 0031  21 loop2:   cmpl     (r6)[r9],min
                   08   18 0036  22           bgeq     after
            5A     59   D0 0038  23           movl     r9,r10
        D4 AF   6649   D0 003B  24           movl     (r6)[r9],min
            ED 59   05   F2 0040  25 after:   aoblss   #n,r9,loop2
                        0044  26           swap     (r6)[r7],(r6)[r10]
        CF AF   6647   D0 0044           movl     (r6)[r7],temp
        6647   664A   D0 0049           movl     (r6)[r10],(r6)[r7]
        664A   C7 AF   D0 004E           movl     temp,(r6)[r10]
                        0053
            CD 57    04   F2 0053  27           aoblss   #n-1,r7,loop1
                   04 0057  28           ret
                        0058  29           .end     start
```

Figure 6–3.

```
00000042 00000009 00000029 00000003 00000003 0000    1 array:  .long   3,9,41,66,3
                                     00000000 0010    2 answer: .long
                                     00000000 0014    3
                                              0018    4         .macro  srchcnt a,n,key,count,?loop,?after
                                              0018    5         moval   a,r6            ;count:= 0
                                              0018    6         clrl    count           ;for i:= 1 to n
                                              0018    7         movzbl  #1,r5           ;if a(i) = key then
                                              0018    8 loop:   cmpl    (r6)+,key
                                              0018    9         bneq    after
                                              0018   10         incl    count           ;count:= count +1
                                              0018   11 after:  aobleq  n,r5,loop
                                              0018   12         .endm
                                              0018   13
                                         0000 0018   14 start:  .word   srchcnt
                                         04   001A   15         srchcnt array,#5,#3,answer
                                              0030   16         ret
                                              0031   17         .end    start
```

Macros vs. MACRO

The word "macro" now has two meanings. We are calling the assembly language itself VAX/MACRO, and there is a construct within the language called a macro (which has been the topic of this chapter). We will distinguish between them by capitalizing the language name, MACRO, and not capitalizing the construct, macro. We will discuss macros further in Chapters 9 and 11.

Exercises

1. What are the advantages of using macros in an assembly language program?

2. What does the *.show me* directive do? What happens if it is not used?

3. What happens at assembly time to a macro call?

4. What two assembler directives define a macro?

5. Write a macro that swaps word 1 with word 2 in a (longword) register.

6. a. Write a macro called *ecount* which searches a string (of up to 30 characters) and counts the number of occurrences of the letter *e*. Store this result in location *count*. *Hint:* Remember each ASCII character is stored in a byte, so byte instructions may be used here. You might want to use

   ```
   e:  .ascii /e/
   ```

   b. Write a main program which uses this macro to store the number of *e*'s in R0. Use

   ```
   string:  .ascii /there are a lot of e's here!/
   ```

   as data. Assemble, link, and run this program. Use the debugger to check the answer.

7. a. Write a macro *itoa* which converts an integer to its ASCII representation.

   b. Write a macro *atoi* which converts the ASCII representation of an integer to its internal representation.

8. Create a file of macros that do some commonly used functions such as computing absolute value, clearing a group of registers, exponentiation, and factorial. Write a program that incorporates these macros and uses them.

9. Write a macro to find the factorial of a number *n* and return the value in R0.

10. The BASIC instruction

   ```
   on x go to label1,label2,label3,  . . .
   ```

   transfers processing to label1, label2, label3, . . . depending on the value of *x*. For example, if *x* = 3, then processing goes to label3, and so forth. Implement a macro called *ongoto* which accepts a longword variable *x* and address labels to transfer to depending on the value of *x*.

Chapter 7

Stacks, Subroutines, and Procedures

7.1 Stacks

A *stack* is a pile or list of items which may be accessed only one at a time and from only one end usually called the *top*. Items are removed from the top and added to the top. Thus, still another name for a stack is a last-in-first-out (LIFO) list. A dishwell in a cafeteria operates as a stack with plates being added and removed from the top of the pile.

The VAX operating system allots a portion of each user's address space as a stack. For the VAX, a stack may be visualized as a consecutive sequence of longwords only one of which may be accessed at a time. Values are stored and removed from the longword at the top of the stack. R14 (also denoted SP) contains the address of the top item in the stack. Initially, before anything is put on the stack, SP contains the address of the bottom of the stack. Of course, initially, the bottom is also the top. As longwords are added to the stack, the addresses *decrease*. Thus if the top of the stack is at location 204, then the next available location is 200 since (1) addresses decrease and (2) each element in the stack is a longword (see Figure 7–1). We write "SP →" to indicate that SP contains the address of (i.e., points to) the top of the stack.

Adding and removing elements from the top of the stack

There are two basic operations on a VAX stack:

1. *Push:* Decrease the stack pointer by 1 longword (4 bytes); then store a longword on the stack.
2. *Pop:* Remove an item from the stack; increase the stack pointer by 1 longword (4 bytes).

97

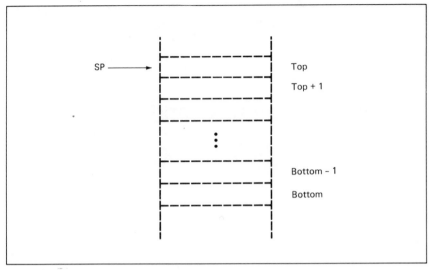

Figure 7–1.

Push instruction

In VAX assembly language, there are two ways to accomplish a push:

```
movl x,-(sp)
```

which pushes value of x onto stack, or

```
pushl x
```

which is equivalent to movl x,–(sp).

There is also a *pusha* instruction which pushes an address onto the stack. To put a 3 onto the top of the stack, write:

```
pushl #3
```

To put the address of list onto the top of the stack, write:

```
pushal list
```

Pop instruction

Pop may be accomplished by:

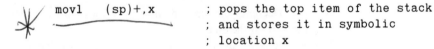

```
movl    (sp)+,x          ; pops the top item of the stack
                         ; and stores it in symbolic
                         ; location x
```

or

```
popl   x                      ;same effect as movl  (sp)+,x
```

EXAMPLE

```
popl rll                ;puts top element of stack into Rll.
```

Pushing and popping registers

Register contents may be pushed onto the system stack by

```
pushl rn
```

where *rn* stands for one of the registers R0–R15, or by

```
pushr <rnl,rn2, . . .>
```

where *rni* again stands for one of the registers R0–R15. Thus

```
pushr <rl,r7,r8>
```

pushes R1, R7, and R8 onto the system stack. The highest-numbered register (here, R8) is pushed onto the stack first regardless of its order in the *pushr* instruction. Similarly,

```
popr <rnl,rn2, . . .>
```

pops the stack contents into the indicated registers, with the first longword going into the lowest-listed register. Thus,

```
popr <r7,rl,r8>
```

pops the first longword on the stack into R1, the next longword on the stack into R7, and the next longword on the stack into R8.

Using stacks

Notice that autodecrement mode is used with a push operation and autoincrement with a pop.

Stacks are often used as a convenient temporary storage area. For example, compilers frequently store arithmetic operands in a stack:

```
pushl a
pushl b
```

Then, when it is time to perform an arithmetic operation, for example $a - b$, the following instruction could be used:

```
subl (sp)+,(sp)
```

(Remember, the first operand is subtracted from the second operand.)

Stacks are also used to access information in reverse order. (The order of the operands in *sub*— and *div*— was specifically designed with stack storage in mind.)

Reversing a list

In Chapter 4 we used a combination of autoincrement and autodecrement to reverse the elements in a list. It is perhaps even easier to reverse a list using a stack. Figure 7–2 is the same program as in Figure 4–8 except that items from *input* are pushed onto the stack one at a time and then popped off one at a time into *output*.

Designing a stack

An assembly language programmer can also design his or her own stack by:

1. Allotting a block of data,
2. Storing the base address in a register, and
3. Using autoincrement and autodecrement modes to pop and push.

EXAMPLE

```
mystack:    .blkb  100 ; allocate 100 bytes
bottom:     .byte      ; and 1 more for the
                       ; bottom
        .
        .
        .
            movab  bottom,r2
      push  movb   item,-(r2)   ; push item onto
                                ; stack
      pop  movb   (r2)+, r9
```

Figure 7–2.

```
input:    .ascii  /abcdefghijklmn/
          endinp = .
start:    .word
          movab   input,r6          ;    while i<= n do
loop1:    cvtbl   (r6)+,-(sp)       ;        push input(i) onto stack
          cmpl    r6,#endinp
          bneq    loop1

          movab   input,r6          ;    while i<= n do
loop2:    cvtlb   (sp)+,(r6)+       ;        pop input(i)  from stack
          cmpl    r6,#endinp
          bneq    loop2
          ret
          .end    start
```

Here *mystack* is a programmer-defined stack of bytes. A programmer-defined stack need not grow to lower addresses. It could grow to "higher" addresses; then autoincrement would be used for a push and autodecrement for a pop.

7.2 Subroutines

Subroutines and procedures are used in assembly language for the same reasons they are used in higher-level languages:

1. They save storage space by branching to a sequence of frequently used code.
2. They help to segment a program, making it easier to code, debug, and maintain.

Subroutine calls involve two essential actions:

1. *Linkage:* Since the subroutine may be called from different places in the program, the subroutine must be given the correct address to return to.
2. *Argument transmission:* The subroutine needs to be able to access the values for its parameters (arguments).

In the VAX, subroutines and procedures are indistinguishable; the linkage and argument transmission are what distinguish them. Subroutine linkage and argument transmission are faster for short routines, but require more work from the programmer than procedure linkage and argument transmission.

Linkage

There are three instructions for transferring to a subroutine:

```
jsb:  jump to subroutine
bsbb: branch to a subroutine which is less than 127 bytes away
bsbw: branch to a subroutine which is less than 32767 bytes away
```

All three of these instructions save the contents of the program counter on the stack before moving the address of the subroutine into the program counter. However, *bsbb* uses less storage space than *bsbw* and *bsbw* uses less than *jsb*.

There is only one instruction for returning from a subroutine:

```
rsb
```

rsb pops the first longword off the stack and loads it into the program counter. If the subroutine also uses the stack, the stack pointer must be reset.

Argument transmission

Arguments may be transmitted three different ways:

1. By placing them in a register.
2. By putting the address of the argument in the stack or a register.
3. By putting them onto the stack.

We will show these three methods of transmitting arguments to call a routine that calculates 2∗3+4:

EXAMPLE (METHOD 1)

```
result: .long
start:  .word
        movl    #2,r1           ; the arguments
        movl    #3,r2           ; are transmitted
        movl    #4,r3           ; via the registers
        bsbb    calc
        ret
calc:   mull2   r1,r2
        addl3   r2,r3,result    ; result:=a∗b+c
        rsb
        .end    start
```

EXAMPLE (METHOD 2)

```
result:     .long
args:       .long   2,3,4   ; arguments
            .long   result  ; answer will be stored
                            ; here
start:      .word
            moval   args,r1
            bsbw    calc
            ret
calc:       mull2   (r1)+,(r1)
            addl3   (r1)+,(r1)+,@(r1)      ; result:=a∗b+c
            rsb
            .end    start
```

EXAMPLE (METHOD 3)

```
result:  .long
start:   .word
         pushal result
         pushl #4
         pushl #3
         pushl #2
         jsb   calc
         addl2 #16,sp    ; restore stack pointer
         ret
calc:    mull2 4(sp),8(sp)
         addl3 8(sp),12(sp),@16(sp)    ; result:=a*b+c
         rsb
         .end  start
```

7.3 Procedures

Procedures are generally indistinguishable from subroutines. The linkage and argument transmission are more sophisticated, however, and do not require as much control from the programmer. There are two instructions for transferring control to a procedure:

> callg: call procedure with *general* argument list
> calls: call procedure with *stack* argument list

and one instruction for returning:

> ret

callg

  callg has two operands. The first operand is the address of the argument list; the second operand is the symbolic name for the procedure.

EXAMPLE

```
    callg args,calc
```

calls procedure *calc* whose arguments are at location *args*.

The argument list must obey the following format: the first longword of the argument list is the number of arguments. The arguments come next, each a longword.

EXAMPLE

```
args:     .long     4       ; there are 4 arguments
          .long     2,3,4   ; they are 2,3,4,
          .long     result  ; and result
```

Register masks

Registers can be automatically saved and restored by using what is called a *mask:*

```
^M<rn 1, rn2,...>
```

where Rn1, Rn2, . . . are the registers to be protected. The mask is the first line of the procedure and is frequently called an *entry mask.*

EXAMPLE

```
calc: .word ^M<r10,r11,r6> ; save R10,R11,R6
```

The argument pointer AP

Before transferring to the procedure, *callg* moves the address of the argument list to R12, the argument pointer (AP). The procedure can then use the AP to access the arguments. Figure 7–3 shows this in procedure *calc*. There, AP

Figure 7–3.

```
result:   .long
args:     .long          4       ; there are 4 arguments
          .long          2,3,4   ; the arguments
          .address       result  ; answer stored in result

start:    .word
          callg          args,calc
          ret

calc:     .word    ^M<r6>
          mull3    4(ap),8(ap),r6
          addl3    r6,12(ap),@16(ap)
          ret
          .end     start
```

contains the address of the number of arguments; hence, (AP) contains 4, the number of arguments passed to procedure *calc*. Then, 4(AP) contains the next argument, the 2, 8(AP) contains the 3, and 12(AP) contains the 4. Since 16(AP) contains the *address* of *result,* we must use "@" to store the calculated value at that address. Thus, we store the value at @16(AP).

calls

calls is similar to *callg* except that the arguments must be first pushed onto the stack. Like *callg, calls* has two operands. The first is the number of operands passed; the second is again the address of the procedure.

EXAMPLE

```
pushal   result
pushl    #4
pushl    #3
pushl    #2
calls    #4,calc
```

When the *calls #4,calc* instruction is executed, the "4" is also pushed onto the stack. Thus (SP) contains this 4. In addition, the argument pointer, AP, is set equal to the stack pointer, SP. Thus, we can use the same procedure *calc* that we used with the *callg*. Figure 7–4 is the same as Figure 7–3 except that the procedure is called via *calls*.

Figure 7–4.

```
result:    .long

start:     .word
           pushal   result    ; answer stored here
           pushl    #4        ;
           pushl    #3        ;these are the arguments
           pushl    #2        ;
           calls    #4,calc
           addl2    #16,sp
           ret

calc:      .word    ^M<r6>
           mull3    4(ap),8(ap),r6
           addl3    r6,12(ap),@16(ap)
           ret
           .end     start
```

7.4   Calling MACRO Procedures from High-level Languages

Introduction

Chapter 1 states reasons for using assembly language rather than machine language. Some of these reasons are:

Operations are mnemonic and easy-to-remember words such as *movl* rather than numeric opcodes such as D0 (or 11010000_2).

Addresses are also symbolic names such as *loop, begin,* and *result* rather than absolutes like 0000000D (or 000. . .1101_2).

A similar and probably longer list could be made stating the reasons for using high-level languages rather than low-level languages like assembly language. In particular, the reader by now realizes that assembly language is somewhat cumbersome. Constructs such as conditionals and loops usually require more code in assembly language than in a higher-level language.

Why, then, do we write in assembly language at all?

Certainly, the compiler writer needs to know how to translate the language he or she is compiling into machine or assembly language. But also, the applications programmer may find that certain sequences of instructions execute faster when written in assembly language—or take up less space, or manage the machine parts such as memory or the I/O devices better. In fact, there are some system routines that can be done only in assembly language. There are, therefore, many reasons for coding in assembly language.

It is not always necessary to write the entire program in assembly language. It is possible to *call* procedures written in one language from procedures or programs written in another language.

Consider, for example, procedure *calc* from the previous examples:

```
calc:     .word     ^M<r6>
          mull3     4(ap),8(ap),r6
          addl3     12(ap),r6,@16(ap)
          ret
```

This procedure can be assembled separately and then *linked* to another assembled or compiled program which calls this procedure. The following shows a FORTRAN program which calls procedure *calc:*

```
      integer a,b,c,result
      read*,a,b,c
      call calc(a,b,c,result)
      write(6,1)result
1     format(i)
      stop
      end
```

FORTRAN, however, passes *addresses*. We passed *values* (for 2, 3, and 4) when we called *calc* via *callg* and *calls*. Thus "@" must be added to access these values in procedure *calc* if it is to be called from FORTRAN this way.

Once these two procedures (the FORTRAN main program and the assembly language procedure) have been compiled and assembled, respectively, they each exist in a form called an *object* module. These object modules are linked together and then the resulting module called the *execution* (or *load*) module may be executed. This entire sequence is shown in Figure 7–5 for the VMS operating system. We will explore this further in Part II.

Figure 7–5.

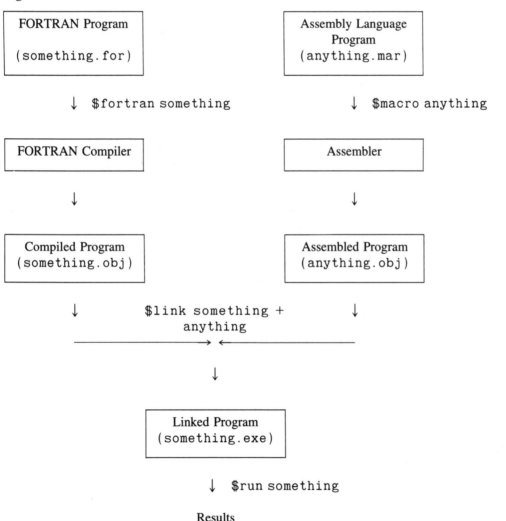

Figure 7–6 shows the steps of Figure 7–5 for the FORTRAN program and procedure *calc*.

:: and ==

In Figure 7–6, note that the assembly language address *calc* is now followed by two colons:

```
calc:: .word ^M<r6>
```

This second colon makes address calc *global,* that is, known to different object modules. Similarly, == is used to assign global values.

EXAMPLE

```
length==10
```

assigns *length* the value of 10 and makes *length* known (as a constant!) to other object modules.

.entry vs. ::

DEC documentation (and many knowledgeable assembly language programmers) prefer the *.entry* statement for linking separate object modules. In our case,

Figure 7–6.

```
$ type callmac.for
        integer a,b,c,result
        read*,   a,b,c
        call    calc(a,b,c,result)
        write(6,1) result
  1     format(i)
        stop
        end
$
$ type calc.mar
calc::  .word   ^M<r6>
        mull3   @4(ap),@8(ap),r6
        addl3   r6,@12(ap),@16(ap)
        ret
        .end
$
$ fortran callmac
$ macro calc
$ link callmac+calc
$ run callmac
2 3 4
        10
FORTRAN STOP
$
```

```
calc::  .word ^M<r6>
```

could be replaced by

```
.entry calc ^M<r6>
```

Registers 0 and 1 need not (in fact may not) be saved since the *entry* statement expects to be able to return values in R0 and R1. Also, *.entry* does not allow R12, R13, R14, and R15 to be masked. Other registers may, however, be masked:

```
.entry calc ^M<r6,r7>
```

is a legal statement.

Despite DEC's recommendation and the fact that the *.entry* statement has other assets (see the VAX-11 *MACRO Language Reference Manual* [18]), we find

```
.entry calc...
```

Figure 7–7.

```
$ type maccall.pas
program callmac(input,output);
var a,b,c,result:integer;
procedure calc(var a,b,c,result:integer);extern;
begin{ callmac }
  writeln('input a,b,c on same line');
  readln(a,b,c);
  calc(a,b,c,result);
  writeln (result)
end{ callmac }.
$
$ type calc.mar
calc::  .word    ^M<r6>
        mull3    @4(ap),@8(ap),r6
        addl3    r6,@12(ap),@16(ap)
        ret
        .end
$
$ pascal maccall
    4               procedure calc(var a,b,c,result:integer);extern;
%PAS-W-DIAGN                                                        ^461
            *** WARNING 461:  Nonstandard Pascal: External procedure decl
 1 Nonstandard feature
$
$ macro calc
$ link maccall+calc
$ run maccall
input a,b,c on same line
2 3 4
        10
$
```

less readable than

```
calc::...
```

The name of the procedure is just not as visible in the *.entry* statement.
Figure 7–7 shows a Pascal main program calling procedure *calc*.

Exercises

1. What is another name for a stack?

2. Why is the stack pointer decreased in a push instruction?

3. Can addresses be stored on the system stack?

4. Where are the contents of the PC saved in a jump to a subroutine using *jsb, bsbb,* and *bsbw*?

5. In what ways are subroutine (and procedures) and macros similar? How are they different?

6. What two actions do subroutine calls invoke?

7. What are the two instructions for transferring control to a procedure?

8. What are the advantages of procedure calls over subroutine calls?

9. What are the three ways that arguments may be transmitted to a procedure?

10. Show the argument transmission and linking for the subroutine example *calc* when the address of the arguments is placed on the stack.

11. Rewrite the program that reverses a list (Figure 7–1) using a programmer-defined stack.

12. Implement the sort program from Chapter 4 as a procedure.

13. Write a subroutine or procedure called *squeez* which eliminates all the blanks in a short line of text. Have your main program call *squeez* with the following data:

```
input: .ascii /a bc d ef g/
```

14. Rewrite the program of Figure 7–2 using macros *pushb* and *popb* which push and pop a byte into and out of a user-defined stack of bytes.

Chapter 8

Input and Output

8.1 Calling High-level Language Procedures for I/O

We have given little attention in this text so far to input and output. Except for Section 7.4, values have been defined inside VAX assembly language programs rather than "read in" as data. Calculated values have not been printed out; instead, Appendix A describes a technique using the (VMS) symbolic debugger. (The debugger can also be used to input values.) Although this may be adequate for many applications, there are other ways of inputting and outputting values. Section 7.4 shows one method of doing this. There, a high-level language reads in the data and prints out the results. The assembly language program does the actual calculation.

Another method is to write the input or output procedure in some favorite high-level language and have the assembly language program call it. Thus, the assembly language program becomes the main program and the high-level language becomes the procedure. This is shown in Figure 8–1, where the FORTRAN subroutines *readval* and *printval* are used to input and output values for the assembly language program *calc*. Similar routines could be written and called in other high-level languages (e.g., BASIC, Pascal).

8.2 Using System Macros for I/O

This section introduces some of the (VMS) system I/O routines. If the VAX you are using has a different operating system from VMS, then this section might reasonably be skipped. These I/O routines are called RMS (for record management services), and only a small subset will be described here. The reader is referred to the *VAX-11 Record Management Services Reference Manual* [26] for a more exhaustive treatment.

As the word *record* in RMS implies, the RMS routines handle I/O in terms of records. We have discovered that where there are records, files are usually lurking. Thus there are operations to open, close, and read from and write onto files. And files consist of related groups of information called records. To define a

Figure 8–1.

```
; This main MACRO program calls two FORTRAN subroutines
; Readval and Printval. Readval reads in the values a,b, and c.
; The MACRO program calculates a*b+c. Then Printval prints
; out result.
;
a:       .long
b:       .long
c:       .long
result:  .long
;
inargs:  .long  3         ; There are 3 input arguments
         .long  a
         .long  b
         .long  c
;
outargs: .long  1         ; There is 1 output argument
         .long  result
;
start:   .word
         callg  inargs,readval
         mull2  a,b
         addl3  b,c,result
         callg  outargs,printval
         ret
         .end   start

         subroutine printval(outval)
         integer outval
         write (6,1) outval
    1    format (' The answer is ',i)
         return
         end
         subroutine readval (a,b,c)
         integer a,b,c
         write (6,1)
    1    format (' Input the values of a, b, and c ')
         read*, a,b,c
         return
         end
```

file, we will need to name it and declare whether we are going to read from it or write onto it; then, for each file we will have to describe its records.

This record description contains the address that the data are to be read into or printed out from and an indication of the size of the data in bytes.

Figure 8–2 shows some of these macros being used in a program whose only function is to print out four asterisks. We will define these macros below. Note that the system macros (the ones beginning with $) are used just like instructions. They are not *linked* since they are part of the operating system.

File and record initialization macros

The first two system macros, *$fab* and *$rab,* are initializing statements. They tell RMS what operations to perform on what records in what files and how to perform them. They are called (user) control blocks and serve (roughly) the same purpose to RMS as data declarations do to the assembler.

$fab is the macro name for a routine that allots a file access block (FAB). A *fab* describes a file and contains such information as the name of the file, the file organization, and the record format. Some useful parameters of *$fab* are

fnm Specifies the name of the file. For example, *fnm=<sys$output>* in Figure 8–2 specifies the system default output device (the terminal for interactive users). The file name is enclosed in ◇'s.

fac Specifies the operations to be performed on the file. *fac=put* means the file is to be used for writing, and *fac=get* means the file is to be used for reading.

The program refers to the *fab* by its label. The label *fab* in Figure 8–2 is *foo.* *$rab* allots and describes a record access block (RAB). Each *fab* has one or more *rab*'s associated with it. Each *rab* must state what *fab* it is associated with and describe the records within the file. Some useful parameters of *$rab* are

fab Specifies the address of the associated *fab;* for example, *fab=foo* says that this *rab* is associated with the *fab* at location *foo.*

Figure 8–2.

```
foo:     $fab      fnm=<sys$output>,fac=put
bar:     $rab      fab=foo,rbf=aster,rsz=4
aster:   .ascii /****/
start:   .word
         $open    fab=foo
         $connect rab=bar
         $put     rab=bar
         $close   fab=foo
         ret
         .end     start
```

rbf Specifies the address of the data to be output. *rbf=aster* in the program in Figure 8–2 states that the data whose value is to be printed out are at location *aster*.

rsz Specifies the record size in bytes of the output. For example, *rsz=4* states that 4 bytes are to be output in the above program. (Remember each ASCII character occupies 1 byte.)

The following parameters are used with input *rab*'s.

ubf Specifies the address into which data are to be read. For example, *ubf=inbuf* indicates that there is a location called *inbuf* into which data is to be input.

usz Specifies the size in bytes of the input data. Care should be taken to be sure the size of the address in the *ubf* is at least as large as the *usz*. For example, *ubf=inbuf, usz=10* would be inconsistent with a declaration

```
inbuf: .blkb 5
```

since the *usz* parameter specifies 10 bytes and the declaration for *inbuf* only allocates 5.

rop Indicates some record-processing options. One option we will use frequently is the option *pmt*, which stands for prompt. Thus *rop=pmt* indicates that a prompt is to be typed out each time this *rab* is used to input. The next parameter is used to describe the actual prompt message to be issued.

pbf Stands for prompt buffer and specifies the address of a prompting message. Thus *pbf=promptmsg* says that there is an address *promptmsg* containing a message to be output before the *rab* accepts input. The declaration for *promptmsg* might be something like

```
promptmsg: .ascii /enter a two-digit number/
```

psz Indicates the size in bytes of the prompt. For the message in *promtmsg* above, *psz=24* since each ASCII character occupies a byte and there are 24 characters between the /'s.

I/O Macros

The following system macros describe the actual operations to be performed on the files and records described in the *$fab* and *$rab* macros.

$open

$open opens a file. A file must, in addition to being declared in *$fab*, be "opened" before any record operations can be performed. Thus

```
$open fab=foo
```

opens the file described in the *fab* at address *foo*.

Figure 8–3.

```
     :
     :       this program demonstrates the use of macro i/o's
     :          to read in three positive integer values, multiplying
     :          the first two, and then adding the third to
     :          obtain the result.
       foo:      $fab       fnm=<sys$input>,fac=get
       bar:      $rab       fab=foo,ubf=inbuf,usz=50
       goo:      $fab       fnm=<sys$output>,fac=put
       gar:      $rab       fab=goo,rbf=outbuf,rsz=12
        k2:      .long      0            ; counter for loopl
   resultl:     .long      0            ; will hold lst number
   result2:     .long      0            ; will hold 2nd number
      divr:      .long      0            ; will hold result
      divd:      .quad      0            ; divd = divr
       quo:      .long      0            ; quotient for ediv
       rem:      .long      0            ; remainder for ediv
     kount:      .long      0            ; count of digits in a number
     inbuf:      .blkb      50           ; input buffer
    outbuf:      .byte      32[12]       ; output buffer
         a:      .byte
     start:      .word
                 $open      fab=foo
                 $connect   rab=bar
                 $open      fab=goo
                 $connect   rab=gar
                 $get       rab=bar
                 movab      inbuf,r6     ; put address of inbuf into r6
                 moval      resultl,r12  ; put address of resultl into r12
     loopl:      clrl       kount        ; kount is no. of digits in number
                 clrl       r7           ; counter for loop2
                 clrl       r8           ; r8 will calculate value of digit
                 clrl       r9           ; r9 will hold value of a number
                 clrl       r10          ; counter for loop3
     check:      cmpb       #32,(r6)     ; is input character a space?
                 beql       space        ; yes, go to space
                 tstb       (r6)         ; is input char a zero?
                 beql       space        ; yes, go to space
                 subb2      #48,(r6)+    ; no, convert char to decimal
                 incl       kount        ; increment kount of digits
                 jmp        check        ; go to check
     space:      mnegl      kount,rll    ; rll =,- (kount)
                 decl       kount        ; kount = kount - 1
                 movab      (r6)[rll],r6 ; r6 gets address of high digit of no.
     loop2:      movzbl     (r6)+,r8     ; r8 gets that digit
                 tstl       kount        ; is kount zero?
                 beql       single       ; yes, so it's a single digit
                 movl       r7,r10       ; r10 gets r7 counter
     loop3:      mull2      #10,r8       ; multiply digit by 10
                 aoblss     kount,r10,loop3  ; need another multiplication?
                 addl2      r8,r9        ; add value of digit to r9
                 aoblss     kount,r7,loop2   ; go get another digit
                 movzbl     (r6)+,r8     ; get last digit into r8
     single:     addl2      r8,r9        ; add last or single digit to r9
                 movl       r9,(r12)+    ; move number to r12 address
                 incl       r6           ; increment to get next char
                 aoblss     #3,k2,loopl  ; get another number
                 mull2      resultl,result2  ; mult the lst two numbers
                 addl2      result2,divr ; add the third number
                 movl       divr,divd    ; must make a quad for ediv
                 movab      a,r12        ; r12 gets address of a
     makasc:     ediv       #10,divd,quo,rem ; start conversion back to ascii
                 movl       quo,divd     ; quo becomes the dividend
                 addb2      #48,rem      ; make rem ascii
                 movb       rem,-(r12)   ; put ascii rem into r12 address
                 tstl       divd         ; out of digits?
                 bneq       makasc       ; get another digit to convert
                 $put       rab=gar      ; output the answer
                 $close     fab=foo
                 $close     fab=goo
     last:       ret
                 .end       start
```

$close

$close terminates the record operations on a file. Thus

```
$close    fab=foo
```

$get

$get is used to input data from a file. For example,

```
$get    rab=inrab
```

will input data as described in the *$rab inrab*. See Figure 8–3.

$put

$put writes a new record to a file. For example,

```
$put    rab=bar
```

outputs the record described in the *rab* at location *bar*. (See Figure 8–3.)

$connect

$connect associates, that is, "connects," a *rab* to a *fab*. It is used after a file has been opened but before any *$get*'s or *$put*'s. In the program in Figure 8–2,

```
$connect    rab=bar
```

connects the opened file with the *rab* at location *bar*.

$disconnect

$disconnect disconnects a *rab* from its associated *fab*.

Figure 8–3 reads in positive integer values for *a, b,* and *c,* calculates

```
result:=a*b+c
```

and writes out the value of *result*.

The length of the program is due primarily to the conversion statements: Characters are input in ASCII and must be converted to internal numeric form. Similarly, in order to output, values must be converted back into ASCII.

8.3   *lib$get_input* and *lib$put_output*

In addition to the RMS macros described in Section 8.2, the VAX/VMS operating system maintains a library of object modules that can be called as procedures. Two particularly useful routines are the procedures *lib$get_input* and *lib$put_output*.

lib$get_input is used to read in a string. *lib$put_output* outputs a string. The rules for using these modules are:

1. The address of the string must be declared using *.ascid*. (For more information on *.ascid*, see the *VAX-Architecture Handbook* [14] and *VAX-MACRO Language Reference Manual* [18].)

EXAMPLE

```
msg:      .ascid      "What is your name?"
```

2. This address is pushed onto the stack before the routine is called.

EXAMPLE

```
pushal msg
```

3. The procedure is then called using *calls*.

EXAMPLE

```
calls   #1,lib$put_output
```

Figure 8–4 illustrates these two procedures.

Figure 8–4.

```
msg1:   .ascid  "What is your name?"
msg2:   .ascid  "Hello, "
name:   .ascid    ""                      ; creates an empty string
;
start:  .word
        pushal  msg1
        calls   #1,lib$put_output
        movw    #80,name                 ; name will be up to 80 chars
        movb    #14,name+2               ; Bookkeeping for the .ascid,
        movb    #2,name+3               ; See Architecture Handbook
        pushal  name
        calls   #1,lib$get_input
        pushal  msg2
        pushal  name
        calls   #1,lib$put_output
        ret
        .end    start
```

Exercises

1. List some differences between RMS and library procedures.

2. Write an assembly language procedure called *type* which outputs the four records contained in a file called *input.dat* (you will have to create such a file) using
   a. RMS
   b. Library procedures

3. Write a procedure to stack input bytes, packing them into a longword. The top longword should contain the number of input characters.

4. What are the limitations of the program in Figure 8–3. That is, what size integers will it handle?

Chapter 9

Writing Good Assembly Language Programs

9.1 Introduction

Designing a good assembly language program is usually more difficult than designing a good high-level language program. (By "good" we mean a correct, efficient, readable, maintainable, etc. program.)

Even designing a good algorithm does not guarantee a good assembly language program design. We saw in Chapter 5 that standard algorithm structures such as *if–then–else* just don't translate in a straightforward way. (Perhaps a different algorithm structure is needed for dealing with assembly languages.)

Data structures must also be implemented in considerably more detail. For example, most high-level languages allow some easy implementation of "an array of integers." But in assembly language a further decision must be made since integers must be specified by size.

Certainly, highly commented programs are a necessity in assembly language. It is not unusual to see an assembly language program with a comment on every line.

In addition, assembly language programs are often implemented using many macros and procedures. This allows a top-down design process and can result in an easier-to-read, easier-to-write assembly language program.

Along with the instruction set, most assembly languages contain another set of directives (sometimes called pseudo-ops). Assembler directives may be regarded as tools which allow the programmer to use the instruction set more effectively. The VAX assembly language has an especially rich set of assembler directives. Section 9.2 will describe some of them.

Another frequently overlooked technique is that of choosing better instructions for the task at hand. For example, the sequence

```
incl a
cmpl a,b
bleq loop
```

can be replaced by the single instruction

```
aobleq b,a,loop
```

Section 9.3 will introduce some instructions which are more appropriate than others we have been using for certain tasks. These are character string instructions and the *case* instruction.

9.2 Assembler Directives

The VAX assembly language consists of two kinds of instructions—the executable instruction set and the assembler directives. The executable instructions (e.g., *movl*) are translated during assembly into machine code, and this machine code is interpreted and acted upon during execution. Assembler directives, on the other hand, are *executed* during the assembly process. They are instructions to the assembler to direct it in its translation. For example,

```
.end
```

tells the assembler that it has reached the end of the program it is translating. Assembler directives in the VAX assembly language begin with ".".

We have already seen many assembler directives: In Chapter 3, data storage directives were described, in Chapter 5 the *.macro* directive was introduced, and in Chapter 6 the *.entry* directive was defined.

This section introduces some other useful assembler directives. The first set of these—*.title, .subtitle, .ident,* and *.psect*—are used for program organization and documentation. The second group, consisting of *.narg, .repeat, .irp, .if,* and *.iif,* are used with *.macro* and vastly increase the power of macros.

Program organization directives

.title

```
.title titlename comment
```

directs the assembler to put the title *titlename* as a heading on the top of each page of the assembly language listing.

EXAMPLE

```
.title   analyze   compares two sorting procedures
```

will generate the title

    `analyze     compares two sorting procedures`

at the top of each page.

Do not confuse the name assigned to the object module in the *.title* directive with the name assigned to the file in which the object module is stored. The command language knows about the file name. The debugger (in VMS) knows about the *.title* name. If none is specified in a *.title*, the VMS debugger calls the object module *.main*.

.subtitle (or *.sbttl*)

A typical assembly language program consists of a number of smaller routines:

    `.subtitle subtitlename comment`

directs the assembler to put *subtitlename* as the second line (under *titlename*) on every page of the listing. This subtitlename appears on each page until the assembler encounters a new *.subtitle*.

EXAMPLE

    `.subtitle   bubblesort   first sort routine`

                    `.`

                    `.`

                    `.`

    `.subtitle   selectionsort next sort routine`

The *.subtitle* directive also causes the assembler to maintain a table of contents. This table of contents contains the *titlename* from *.title* and the names from any *.subtitles* and is printed on the first page of the assembly language listing.

.ident

The *.title* directive names an object module. Frequently, programs are changed—either because they didn't work correctly or because some modifications are desired. The programmer may want to keep the same *.title* name, but at the same time want to attach some indication that this version differs from previously assembled modules with the same *(.title)* name.

    `.ident string`

includes the characters in *string* in the assembly language listing.

EXAMPLE

    `.title analyze`
    `.ident "version 2"`

will cause

```
analyze
version 2
```

to be written on each page of the listing.

.psect

.title, .subtitle, and *.ident* direct the assembler to label different sections of the same object module.

```
.psect name
```

directs the assembler to create a new program section. Each time the assembler encounters a *.psect* with a new name, it sets a location counter to 0 to begin the translation. If the assembler encounters a *.psect* with the same name as a previous *.psect,* it continues its translation from where it left off. Thus the assembler maintains as many location counters as there are program sections with different names. Different *.psects* frequently are used to separate data from instructions. The linker links the separate program sections into one executable module. (It does this automatically—we don't have to specify the program sections in the *link* command).

We can specify execution options called program section *attributes* in a *.psect.* These attributes are optional and are listed after the *.psect* name:

```
.psect name,list of attributes
```

EXAMPLE

```
.psect    data, noexe,wrt
```

Here, the name of the program section is *data*. During execution, this section may not be executed *(noexe);* that is, it contains no executable instructions. The contents of this program section may, however, be written into *(wrt);* that is, the contents of the various addresses may be changed during execution. Such a program section quite likely contains data declarations (e.g., *a: .long 2*). An executable program section might reasonably be assigned the attributes for execution *(exe)* and nonmodification *(nowrt)*.

The interested reader should see the VAX-11 *MACRO Language Reference Manual* [18] for a complete list of *.psect* attributes and the VAX-11 *MACRO Language Users Guide* [19] for a description of their use.

The VMS debugger uses the name in a *.psect* to identify the program section being examined.

Organizing an assembly language program

The assembler directives described here are used to organize and document assembly language programs. They enable a program to be modularized, that is, separated into smaller logical units. Using them makes an assembly language program easier to code, debug, change, and maintain.

Macros also allow us to visualize a program as a collection of logical units. The next section describes some assembler directives that are frequently used in conjunction with macros. Some of them may be used only within macros. Figure 9–1 shows the same program as Figure 5–3 except that organizational directives have been added.

Macro directives

.narg

The number of actual arguments handed to a macro may be less than the number of formal arguments. In such cases we can "discover" how many actual arguments are handed to the macro.

```
.narg symbolname
```

assigns to *symbolname* the number of actual arguments specified in the macro call.

Figure 9–1.

```
        .title   pseudo  program to demonstrate pseudo-ops
        .ident   "version 2"
        .psect   data,noexe,wrt
a:      .long    3,9,41,66,3
        n = <.-a>/4
key:    .long    3
count:  .long


        .psect   code,exe,nowrt
start:  .word
        moval    a,r6
        clrl     count             ; count := 0
        movzbl   #1,r5             ; loop for i := 1 to n
loop:   cmpl     (r6)+,key         ;   if a(i) = key
        bneq     after
        incl     count             ;      then count := count + 1
after:  aobleq   #n,r5,loop        ; end loop
        ret
        .end     start
```

EXAMPLE

```
        .macro   push$    a1,a2,a3,a4,a5,a6,a7,a8,a9,a10
          .narg    x
             .

             .

             .

        .endm    push$
;
start:    .word
          push$    r0,r1,r2
             .

             .

             .

          push$    r5
```

In the first macro call *(push$ r0,r1,r2)*, the symbol *x* is assigned the value 3 since there are three arguments; the second call *(push$ r5)* assigns the value 1. *.narg* may be used only within a macro. Remember that in both cases, the value of *x* is evaluated during assembly. These values are constants during execution.

.if

A sequence of instructions may be assembled or not assembled based upon the outcome of a condition.

```
.if    condition    argument(s)
          .

          .

          .

 .endc
```

assembles the statements between the *.if* and *.endc* only if the specific condition is met.

EXAMPLE

```
.if eq x
     clrl −(sp)
.endc
```

assembles the instruction *clrl −(sp)* only if *x* is equal to 0.

Other condition tests are

```
.if ne         expression       ; if expression is nonzero
.if gt(lt)     expression       ; if expression is greater than
                                ; (less than) zero
.if df(ndf)    symbolname       ; if symbolname is (is not) defined
.if b(nb)      argumentname     ; if argumentname is (is not) blank
.if idn(dif)   argl,arg2        ; if argl is identical to (different
                                ; from) arg2
```

.iif

If only one instruction is to be assembled conditionally, then there is a short form available:

```
.iif condition  argument(s),statement
```

EXAMPLE

```
.iif eq x, clrl −(sp)
```

is equivalent to the code in the previous example. *.if* and *.iif* may be used outside of macros.

.repeat (or *.rept*)

It is possible to repeat the expansion of a sequence of instructions:

```
.rept      expression
   .
   .
   .
.endr
```

evaluates *expression* and assembles the statements represented by the three dots as many times as the value of *expression*.

EXAMPLE

```
.macro·    makeword,n
   .rept   n
      .word
   .endr
.endm
```

will assemble to

```
.makeword   3
    .repeat   3
        .word
    .endr
    .word
    .word
    .word
```

if the macro is called with

```
makeword    3
```

.irp

It is possible to repeat the expansion of a sequence of instructions indefinitely. At the same time each expansion can cause a different argument to be included.

```
.irp    symbolname,<argument list>
    .
    .
    .
    .endr
```

causes the code represented by the three dots to be repeated as many times as there are arguments in the argument list. Each expansion assigns to *symbolname* the next value in the argument list.

The following example illustrates *.irp* (as well as some of the previous directives). It is a macro which pushes up to 10 arguments onto the stack.

```
.macro    push$    a1,a2,a3,a4,a5,a6,a7,a8,a9,a10
    .narg     x
    .iif    eq x,    clrl  -(sp)
    .irp a, <a1,a2,a3,a4,a5,a6,a7,a8,a9,a10>
        .iif eq x,    .mexit
        .iif b a,    clrl  -(sp)
        .iif nb a    pushl a
        x=x-1
    .endr
.endm
```

(*.mexit* terminates the macro expansion just as though *.endm* were encountered.) Figure 9–2 shows an assembly language program using the above macro. Figure 9–3 is the assembled version showing the macro expansions.

Note that where the macro *push$* is invoked, it is first listed with the actual arguments which are substituted for the formal parameters; then it is expanded.

There are other assembly language directives useful for controlling macro expansions, and the serious assembly language programmer should be aware of them.

9.3 More Advanced Instructions

Character string instructions

We can perform operations on sequences of characters (character strings) by using byte instructions since each ASCII character is stored in a byte. VAX assembly language, however, contains a set of instructions to be used specifically with character strings. Using one of these instructions, it is possible to move an entire sequence of characters with one instruction. Another of these instructions can be used to find a particular character within a sequence of characters. Still another instruction can be used to compare two sequences of characters. Some of the instructions use Registers 0–5 to return values; thus these registers must be used with care in a program containing character string instructions.

Moving character strings

```
movc3 length,string1,string2   ;moves length characters from
                                ;address string1 to address
                                ;string2.
```

Figure 9–2.
```
.macro   push$   a1,a2,a3,a4,a5,a6,a7,a8,a9,a10
  .narg    x
  .iif   eq x,   clrl  -(sp)
  .irp   a, <a1,a2,a3,a4,a5,a6,a7,a8,a9,a10>
    .iif    eq x,   .mexit
    .iif    b a,    clrl -(sp)
    .iif    nb a,   pushl a
    x=x-1
  .endr
.endm
start:  .word
.show me
        push$   r5
        push$   r5,r6
        .end    start
```

Figure 9–3.

```
          0000     1  .macro   push$   a1,a2,a3,a4,a5,a6,a7,a8,a9,a10
          0000     2    .narg   x
          0000     3    .iif    eq x,   clrl  -(sp)
          0000     4    .irp    a,  <a1,a2,a3,a4,a5,a6,a7,a8,a9,a10>
          0000     5      .iif   eq x,   .mexit
          0000     6      .iif   b a,    clrl  -(sp)
          0000     7      .iif   nb a,   pushl a
          0000     8      x=x-1
          0000     9    .endr
          0000    10  .endm
  0000    0000    11  start:  .word
          0002    12  .show me
          0002    13          push$   r5
00000001  0002          .narg   x
          0002          .iif    eq x,   clrl  -(sp)
          0002          .irp    a,  <r5,,,,,,,,,>
          0002            .iif   eq x,   .mexit
          0002            .iif   b a,    clrl  -(sp)
          0002            .iif   nb a,   pushl a
          0002            x=x-1
          0002          .endr
          0002            .iif   eq x,   .mexit
          0002            .iif   b r5,   clrl  -(sp)
  55  DD  0002            .iif   nb r5,  pushl r5
00000000  0004            x=x-1
          0004
          0004            .iif   eq x,   .mexit
          0004
          0004    14          push$   r5,r6
00000002  0004          .narg   x
          0004          .iif    eq x,   clrl  -(sp)
          0004          .irp    a,  <r5,r6,,,,,,,>
          0004            .iif   eq x,   .mexit
          0004            .iif   b a,    clrl  -(sp)
          0004            .iif   nb a,   pushl a
          0004            x=x-1
          0004          .endr
          0004            .iif   eq x,   .mexit
          0004            .iif   b r5,   clrl  -(sp)
  55  DD  0004            .iif   nb r5,  pushl r5
00000001  0006            x=x-1
          0006
          0006            .iif   eq x,   .mexit
          0006            .iif   b r6,   clrl  -(sp)
  56  DD  0006            .iif   nb r6,  pushl r6
00000000  0008            x=x-1
          0008
          0008            .iif   eq x,   .mexit
          0008
          0008    15          .end    start
```

After execution of *movc3*, registers R0, R2, R4, and R5 equal 0; R1 contains the address *string1 + length;* R3 contains the address *string2 + length.*

EXAMPLE

```
     name:    .ascii    /Johnson/
  newname:    .blkb     10
    start:    .word
              movc3     #5,name,newname
```

moves the characters "Johns" to *newname.*

In

```
movc5 length1,string1,fillchar,length2,string2
```

movc5 is similar to *movc3* except that it is used when the length of *string1* differs from the length of *string2. fillchar* is used if *length1* < *length2.* If *length1* > *length2,* then only *length2* characters from *string1* are moved.

EXAMPLE

```
     name: .ascii /Johnson/
  newname: .blkb  10
    start: .word
           movc5 #5,name,#^A/ /,#10,newname
```

puts "Johns   " into *newname* since the 5 characters moved are padded with blanks.

Comparing two character strings

There are also two instructions for comparing one sequence of characters with another sequence of characters—one where both strings are of the same length and one where they are of different lengths.

```
cmpc3 length,string1,string2  ;compares length characters
                              ;starting at address string1
                              ;with length characters
                              ;starting at address string2.
```

After this instruction is executed, R0 contains 0 if the two strings are equal; otherwise R0 contains the number of bytes left in *string1* starting with the first character that differed. R1 contains the address of this first differing character in *string1;* if they are the same, R1 contains the address one byte beyond *string1.* R3 contains the same information as R1 except that it is for *string2.* R2 equals R0.

Example

```
name1:   .ascii   /Johns/
name2:   .ascii   /Johnson/
start:   .word
         cmpc3    #5,name1,name2
         beql     equal
```

After the *cmpc3* instruction is executed, control will pass to label *equal* since the first five characters in *name1* and *name2* are the same.

```
cmpc5 length1,string1,fillchar,length2,string2
```

is the same as *cmpc3* except that the fill character *(fillchar)* is appended to the shorter character string if the strings are equal up to that point. After execution, R0 contains 0 if (1) *string1* and *string2* are of equal length and they contain the same characters or (2) *length1* < *length2* and *string1* is the same as *string2* up to *length1*; otherwise R0 contains the number of bytes left in *string1* starting with the first differing character. R2 is the same as R0, but for *string2*. R1 and R3 are the same as for *cmpc3*.

Example

```
name1:   .ascii   /Johnson/
name2:   .ascii   /Johns/
start:   .word
         cmpc5    #7,name1,#^A/ /,#5,name2
         bleq     first
```

This *cmpc5* instruction compares "Johnson" with "Johns". Since "o" is not less than or equal to " " (i.e., blank), control will not pass to label *first*.

Searching character strings

It is possible to search through character strings looking for the first appearance *(locc)* or nonappearance *(skpc)* of a particular character (called *key* below).

```
locc key,length,string   ;searches length characters starting
                         ;at address string for the first
                         ;occurrence of key.
```

After execution of *locc*, R0 contains the number of bytes remaining in the string if *key* was found or 0 if it was not found. R1 contains the address of *key* in *string* if found; otherwise R1 contains the address of *string* + *length*.

```
skpc key,length,string   ;is the same as locc except it looks for the
                         ;first nonoccurrence of key starting
                         ;at address string.
```

EXAMPLE

```
text:   .ascii  /    This is the beginning /
start:  .word
        skpc    #^A/ /,#20,text
        locc    #^A/i/,#20,text
```

After *skpc* is executed, Register 1 will contain the address of *text+4*, since that is where the first nonblank occurs. After *locc* is executed, Register 1 will contain the address *text+6* since this is where the first "i" occurs.

Finding substrings

locc is used to search through a string for a single character. The following instruction is used to search through a string looking for a sequence of consecutive characters (a substring):

```
matchc length1,string1,length2,string2 ;searches length2
                                        ;characters starting at
                                        ;address string2 for
                                        ;the first occurrence
                                        ;of length1 characters
                                        ;starting at address
                                        ;string1.
```

After execution of *matchc*, R0 contains 0 if no match occurred; otherwise R0 contains the number of characters remaining in *string2* including the substring length *(length1)* if a match occurred. R1 contains 0 if there was no match; otherwise R1 contains the address in *string2* where *string1* begins.

EXAMPLE

```
keyword:  .ascic   /begin/
  prose:  .ascic   /As it was in the beginning, is now.../
  start:  .word
          movab    keyword,r7
          movb     (r7)+,r8    ; move length of keyword
          movab    prose,r9
          movb     (r9)+,r10   ; move length of prose
          matchc   r8,(r7),r10,(r9)
```

After *matchc* is executed, Register 1 contains the address *prose + 17* which is where the string *begin* starts.

Case instruction

In high-level languages which support it, the *case* instruction is used when there are more than two outcomes of a condition (so that *if–then–else* is not sufficient):

```
           case selector of
    valuel: statements
              .
              .
              .

    value2: statements
              .
              .
              .

    value3: statements
              .
              .
              .

           end case
```

The way this statement works is as follows: *selector* is evaluated and if it equals *value1*, then the statements at *value1* are evaluated; if *selector* equals *value2*, then the statements at *value2* are evaluated; and so forth.

The FORTRAN *computed goto* is essentially a *case* statement. In fact, it seems to be the motivation for the VAX assembly language *case* statement. In FORTRAN

```
    go to (10,20,30,...)I
```

would cause execution to transfer to label 10 if $I = 1$, to label 20 if $I = 2$, and so on.

The form for the *case* statement in VAX assembly language is:

```
        case selector,base,limit     ; base<=selector<=base+limit
;
label:  displacement 0               ; if selector=base go to label
                                     ; +displacement 0
        displacement 1               ; if selector=base+1 go to
                                     ; label+displacement 1
           .
           .
           .
        displacement base+limit      ; if selector=base+limit go to
                                     ; label+displacement base+limit
```

EXAMPLE

```
    go to (10,20,30,40,50)I
```

would be

```
            casel   i,#1,#4          ; i goes from 1 to 5 (1+4!)
    ;
    table:  .word   10$-table        ; if i=1 go to 10$
            .word   20$-table        ; if i=2 go to 20$
            .word   30$-table        ; if i=3 go to 30$
            .word   40$-table        ; if i=4 go to 40$
            .word   50$-table        ; if i=5 go to 50$
            (ends up here if i is some other value)
```

The following program uses a *case* statement.

A program

Problem: Write a procedure which accepts three arguments: integers x and y and an operator *op* where

$$op = 1 \text{ for addition}$$
$$op = 2 \text{ for multiplication}$$
$$op = 3 \text{ for subtraction}$$
$$op = 4 \text{ for division}$$

and computes the appropriate sum, product, difference, or quotient.

Discussion: Since there are four choices for *op,* a case statement will be appropriate here. The program is shown in Figure 9–4.

9.4   Reentrancy and Recursion

Reentrant procedures

The VAX is primarily a time-sharing system. Many users may be "logged on" at one time, sharing the resources of the computer. These resources may consist of software (i.e., programs) as well as hardware components such as printers, and so on. In particular, editors, compilers, and other systems programs are shared. To give each user his or her own copy of such large programs is much too space-consuming. Instead, a single copy of the executable code is kept and each user executes this single copy. Usually, more than one user may execute the program at a time. Such a program is called reentrant. Because there is only one copy of the program, care must be taken that it is not changed in any way. Thus there is no modifiable data section (see Section 9.2) in such a program. Instead, registers and the system stack are used to provide the data for reentrant programs. Thus if we wish to *write* reentrant procedures, we must store local data in registers or in the stack and pass parameters via the registers or the stack.

Figure 9–4.

```
            .title   Case      program to illustrate the case statement
            .subtitle          .main.   main program

                  .psect   data,noexe,wrt           ; data section

  x:                .long    10                      ; argument 1
  y:                .long    2                       ; argument 2
  op:               .long    4                       ; operator
  ans:              .long                            ; result

                  .psect   code,exe,nowrt            ; code section

  start:            .word                            ; beginning of program

                  pushal  ans                        ; push addresses
                  pushal  op                         ; of all arguments
                  pushal  y                          ; onto stack,
                  pushal  x                          ; and call procedure
                  calls   #4,compute                 ; with 4 arguments
;           ans should now contain 5 (10/2),
;           and r1 should contain 0

                  ret                                ; end of program

;- - - - - - - - - - - - - - - - - - - - - - - - - - - - - - - - - - - -
        .subtitle          compute procedure to compute ANS from X Y and OP;
; Procedure to calculate a 2-term equation (callable as external function)
; Arguments are:  X, Y, OP, and ANS
;     (addresses held in 4(ap), 8(ap), 12(ap), and 16(ap), respectively)
; Error code is returned in r0     {if r0 = 0 then o.k., if r0 = 1 error}
  compute::         .word
                  movl    #1,r0                      ; set r0 to one (success)
                  casel   @12(ap),#1,#3              ; 1 <= op <=4
  table:            .word    10$ – table             ; op = 1
                    .word    20$ – table             ; op = 2
                    .word    30$ – table             ; op = 3
                    .word    40$ – table             ; op = 4
; if op is not a known value, drop through to here
                  clrl    r0                         ; signal error
                  ret                                ; and exit
; else, select one of the following:

  10$:              add13   @8(ap),@4(ap),@16(ap) ; ans = x + y
                    ret
  20$:              sub13   @8(ap),@4(ap),@16(ap) ; ans = x – y
                    ret
  30$:              mul13   @8(ap),@4(ap),@16(ap) ; ans = x * y
                    ret
  40$:              div13   @8(ap),@4(ap),@16(ap) ; ans = x / y
                    ret
; end of procedure
                  .end     start
```

Figure 9–5.

```
          .title  expression       a recursion example
          .subtitle         .main.  main program
:
: program to use procedure expr to validate an expression string
:
string: .byte    0[80]            : input string (may be 80 characters)
length: .long                     : variable to hold length of string
valid:  .long                     : variable to hold validation
:
start:  .word                     : start of main program
        pushal  length            : push address of arg 2 (length)
        pushab  string            : push address of arg 1 (string)
        calls   #2,getstr         : call fortran sub. to read in string
:
        pushal  length            : push address of argument 2 (length)
        pushab  string            : push address of argument 1 (string)
        calls   #2,expr           : call procedure expr to validate string
:
        movl    r0,valid          : put r0 into valid
:
        pushal  valid             : push address of arg 1 (valid)
        calls   #1,putval         : call fortran sub. to print valid
:
        ret                       : exit main program
:
: end of main program
:
:
          .subtitle       expr     expression evaluator
:
: procedure expr to validate an expression string
:
: arguments: base address of string, and address of length of string
:
newlen: .long                     : local variable for offset
:
expr::  .word    ^M<r3,r4,r5>     : mask to save three registers
:
        movl     4(ap),r3         : address of string
        movl     (a 8(ap),r4      : length of string
        decl     r4               : convert length to offset
        movl     r4,newlen        : copy of offset
:
        clrl     r0               : set to invalid
        movb     (r3)[r4],r5      : put last character into r5
        tstl     r4               : compare offset to 1
        blss     finish           : exit if empty string
        bgtr     big              : skip to big if longer than 1 character
:
: string is only one character long – check to see if it is a letter
:
short:  cmpb     r5,#^A/A/        : compare to "A"
        blssu    finish           : exit if less than "A"
        cmpb     r5,#^A/Z/        : compare to "Z"
        bgtru    finish           : exit if greater than "Z"
        movl     #1,r0            : string is valid, set r0 to valid,
        ret                       : and exit
:
```

(continued)

```
; string is longer than 1 character - check to make sure last char. is a
; letter or a digit and then (if it is ok) call expr to check rest of string
;
big:      cmpb    r5,#^A/A/         ; compare to "A"
          blssu   digit             ; skip to digit if less than "A"
          cmpb    r5,#^A/Z/         ; compare to "Z"
          blequ   rest              ; skip to rest if less than or equal to "Z"
digit:    cmpb    r5,#^A/0/         ; compare to "0"
          blssu   finish            ; exit if less than "0"
          cmpb    r5,#^A/9/         ; compare to "9"
          bgtru   finish            ; exit if greater than "9"
;
; last char. is valid - call expr to check rest of string (i.e. use offset
; as length parameter)
;
rest:     pushl   newlen            ; push local variable onto stack before call
;
          pushal  newlen            ; push address of argument 2 (length)
          pushl   r3                ; push address of argument 1 (string)
          calls   #2,expr           ; call expr with above 2 arguments
;
          movl    (sp)+,newlen      ; pop local variable off stack after call
;
finish:   ret                       ; exit (call has set r0 appropriately)
;
; end of procedure expr
;
          .end    start
```

Figure 9–5 (*continued*).

Recursive procedures

A special kind of reentrant procedure is one which reenters itself. Such procedures are called *recursive*. Thus, procedure A may, in the process of execution call procedure A. Frequently, such a call is followed by more instructions so that it is expected that the *called* procedure A will return to the *caller* procedure A. Certainly, such procedures must save the return address somewhere. A called procedure returns to its caller; thus when the called procedure returns, it is to the address following the call. If the calling procedure were itself called, then we now need the address to which it is to return. Since we are accessing these addresses in a last-saved, first-unsaved fashion, the stack is a reasonable place to save these addresses. The instructions *calls* and *ret* automatically save and unsave (respectively) the return address. Thus these instructions can be used to solve the problem of the return address. To preserve the value of any values stored in registers, we can use a *mask* (see Section 7.4). And local variables can be pushed onto the stack before the *calls* instruction is executed. Perhaps the best way to understand these ideas is to look at a recursive program.

A recursive program

Problem: Write a recursive program which returns a value of 1 in R0 if a character string represents a "legal identifier" and a value of 0 in R0 if it does not.

Discussion: An identifier may be defined as follows:

$s_1 s_2 s_3 s_4 \ldots s_n$ is an identifier if:

a. $n = 1$ and s_1 is a letter, and
b. s_n is a letter or a digit and $s_1 s_2 s_3 \ldots s_{n-1}$ is an identifier.

Thus a character string is an identifier if it begins with a letter and is followed by a sequence of letters or digits. Many programming languages define identifiers similarly. Thus, *a, x, a1, r2d2,* and *loop* are all legal identifiers while *3, 2rdr,* and *1x* are not. We will not make any restrictions on the length of the identifier here (although we must in reality make some limit!). The procedure is shown in Figure 9–5.

Exercises

1. Put documentation directives into the programs you have written.

2. Rewrite macro *ecount* (exercise 6, Chapter 6) using character string instructions.

3. Define a macro called *blkw_init* which is invoked with one parameter, *p1*, and one optional parameter, *p2*, that will assemble *p2* identical *.word* directives each initializing a word of storage to the same value *p1*. If *p2* is left blank in the actual call to *blkw_init*, then only one word of storage is to be initialized to *p1*. Assume *p1* and *p2* are values known at assembly time. Write the program 2 different ways:
   a. Use *.blkb* inside *blkw_init*.
   b. Do not use *.blkb* inside *blkw_init*. (Use *.rept n . . . .endr*.)

4. Write a macro called *if* which simulates a high-level language *if* statement. For example,

```
if x,lt,y,label
```

   might cause control to pass to *label* if $x < y$. Make your macro as general as possible. Can you write a single macro that will allow other relations besides *lt* and still work correctly?

5. Extend exercise 4 to simulate an *if–then–else* statement.

6. Write a recursive procedure that will write out all the permutations of a set of letters. For example, the permutations of

```
letters: .ascii /abc/
```

   are *abc, acb, bac, bca, cab, cba.*

7. Write recursive procedures *itoa* and *atoi* (see exercise 7, Chapter 6).

8. Rewrite exercise 10 of Chapter 6 using a *case* instruction.

9. The Pascal statement

```
        case control of
1:          a:=1;
2,3,4:      a:=control;
otherwise   a:=0;
```

evaluates the variable *control*. If the value of *control* is 1, then *a:=1* is executed; if *control* = 2, 3, or 4, then *a:=control* is executed. Otherwise *a:=0* is executed. Code this into VAX assembly language.

10. Write a macro which uses the character string instructions introduced in this chapter to count the number of characters in a string and restores the registers before exiting.

Part II

VAX/MACRO Systems Issues

Chapter 10

Assembler Design Issues

10.1 Introduction

In this chapter we wish to study some of the issues related to the software design of assemblers. Given the familiarity that the reader has with VAX/MACRO at this point we will focus on the problem of "writing" an assembler for the VAX/MACRO language.

In this development, "writing" does not mean producing working code. What it does mean is the following:

Identifying key design issues, employing a modular software design philosophy.
Specifying, from a functional point of view, the operation of each module.
Leading the reader, through the Exercises, to greater levels of implementation detail.

We will view VAX/MACRO, for the purposes of the discussions to follow, as having three types of features: *intrinsic features, global features,* and *macro facility features*. The intrinsic features of VAX/MACRO are defined in a negative sense—they are those features that do not relate to either global symbol considerations or to macro considerations.

We will view the assembler design problem as one that is concerned with the intrinsic features of VAX/MACRO. To avoid cluttering up our discussion with a myriad of "essential" but unilluminating details, we will simplify our view of the VAX/MACRO language; that is, we will not try to deal with everything in this development. For example we shall not consider I/O issues at all and will ignore local symbols (labels) and conditional assembly. Appendix B more clearly indicates what design issues we are overlooking. The reader will be asked to examine them further in the Exercises to Appendix B.

Appendix C introduces a subset of VAX/MACRO suitable for student assembler design, to be used as the basis for a student project.

10.2   The Assembler Problem in General Terms

We can all give a quick, simple definition of what an *assembler* is; after all we have all used one on many occasions. An assembler is a (system) program that "translates" assembly language into something called "object code." Because the assembler is a program and involves considerable character manipulation and address manipulation, the assembler itself is often written in assembly language.

The purpose of this section is to reexamine what we mean by "translate" into "object code." Let us first deal with the question of what object code consists of:

Machine code
Listings
Error diagnostics

These items (and possible others) comprise an object file although the listings and diagnostics are often physically part of a separate "list" file. Let us investigate the parts of this file a little further. The concept of machine code is fairly intuitive—it is a set of ordered pairs of the form

(virtual memory location, byte contents)

Note that we have not defined the exact format of this pair, and we will not do so. Listings are also familiar objects. Among the things included in the listing part of the object file are

The source statements themselves, usually with line numbers attached to them.
All generated instructions or data, in hexadecimal for VAX/MACRO, along with
   their addresses; that is, the machine code, in ASCII, appears in the listing.
User supplied headings and subheadings.
Optionally, tables of symbols and their values and, often, from where they are
   referenced.
Error messages; that is, the error diagnostics appear in the listing.

The diagnosis of errors is an important part of the assembly process and the recording of error messages takes place in the listing part of the object file.

The need for more organization

In this section we would like to solidify some key concepts. In order to do this we will need to specify algorithms in some very general, high-level terms. How?

There is considerable variation among authors currently in the matter of algorithm specification. Flowcharts have been a traditional means for specifying computational features; they have the advantage of being language-independent and graphical (visual) in structure. However they are time-consuming to draw and too often, due to a proliferation of loops, are hard to implement and can lead to inefficient code. In the past few years authors have begun to replace flowcharts with higher-level pseudo-languages containing block structures and IF–THEN–ELSE constructs (as in Part I of the text). This has the advantage of producing more structured higher-level programs. Its principal disadvantages stem from having to learn a specialized syntax for algorithm specification. (We saw, as well, in Chapter 5, that many of these constructs do not implement well into assembly language.)

For these and other reasons we will express algorithms in this and the following two chapters in an intuitive English-language form. Our goal in this presentation is not so much that of precision of specification, but of discussion of ideas. In particular, then, our specifications will probably have to be recouched in a more formal setting, prior to coding.

The two-pass assembler concept

In order to produce object code the assembler must, among other things, define values for all symbols appearing in the source program. There are two generic types of symbols in VAX/MACRO: permanent symbols and user-defined symbols. The permanent symbols are the operation mnemonics, the assembler directives, the register names, and so on. The assembler can easily define the values of these symbols (we explore the concept of "value" further below) by consulting prestored decoding tables. It is the user-defined symbols, the ones that vary from program to program, that present the problem. They have no intrinsic values, but have values that depend upon where they occur in the source program and how they are used.

Because forward references to such symbols can appear in the operand field of instructions, it is very difficult to generate machine code in a single scan or pass of the source program. (The reader should write a simple VAX/MACRO program containing forward references to convince him- or herself of the problems related to single-pass assembly; forward references create the need for default conventions in addressing modes as well, to allow the location counter to be properly adjusted during the assembly process.)

The assembler we will describe in this chapter is thus based on the two-pass concept. The goals of the passes are as follows:

Pass 1: Evaluate all user-defined symbols.
Pass 2: Evaluate all permanent symbols and generate object code.

Error diagnosis occurs in both passes in general.

The location counter and symbol evaluation

We recall from our experience with VAX/MACRO that the value of a user-defined symbol defined as a label is that of the current value of the location counter. Remember that due to the virtual address nature of the VAX we may assume that all VAX/MACRO programs begin assembly with the location counter (LC) set to 0. (We will not be involved with .*psect*'s or other location counter–related concepts in this chapter.) As we have no explicit mechanism for changing the location counter (other than the .= assignment statement), only implicit changes occur to it as each line of source code is processed. We refer to this process below as LC adjustment.

Let us give a very-high-level algorithm to summarize the assembly process.

Pass 1:

1. Set LC = 0
2. Read a line of source code.
3. Decode from free format to fixed format.
4. What type of statement is it?
    4.1. .*end*? Go to Pass 2.
    4.2. An assignment statement? Evaluate the expression and either enter the symbol and its value into the symbol table or adjust LC. Go to 2. (*Note:* It is only for the .= *xxx* statement that the LC must be adjusted.)
    4.3. Label present? If so, set it equal to LC and enter its value into the symbol table.
    4.4. Machine instruction? Compute needed size in bytes (using default conventions if necessary) and adjust LC. Go to 2.
    4.5. Assembler directive? Compute needed size in bytes and adjust LC. Go to 2.
    4.6. Comment? Go to 2.
    4.7. If we make it here, there is an error. Process the error. Go to 2.

Pass 2:

1. Set LC = 0.
2. Read a line of source code. Insert into proper field of listing line.
3. Using decoded form of statement from Pass 1, what type of statement is it?
    3.1. .*end*? Go to *exit*.
    3.2. Assignment statement? If of type *symbol=xxx*, go to 4. Otherwise it is a statement of the form .=*xxx*. Evaluate the expression and adjust LC. Go to 4.
    3.3. Machine instruction? Evaluate operation code and all operands using addressing modes, symbol table searches, expression evaluation, and permanent symbol values. Place machine code into proper field of listing line, and into object file. Adjust LC. Go to 4.
    3.4. Assembler directive? Perform required function (data generation if needed). Output such data, if created, to object file with LC value. Place into listing line. Adjust LC. Go to 4.

3.5. Comment? Go to 4.

3.6. If we make it here, there is an error. Process it. Go to 4.

4. Based upon listing control parameters, output listing line. Go to 2.

We have ignored many issues of error diagnosis here and have done so deliberately. We explore these further in the following section. (Before beginning section 10.3, the reader should attempt the exercises for this section, particularly exercise 4.)

10.3 Modular Design Issues for Assemblers

Based upon our discussion to this point and our knowledge of assembly language, we can identify the need for the following modules in our assembler design (there is no significance to their ordering):

I/O module

Decoder from free-format module

Table entry/search module

Location counter adjustment module

Error handler module

Assembler directive processor module (contains submodules)

Machine code generator module

Expression evaluation module

Listing module

Each of the above modules may be subdivided to some degree, and one can add to this list modules that coordinate calls to the above modules (i.e., executive modules). How does one know when to stop subdividing modules? What are the advantages of modular design? The disadvantages? We address some of these issues below.

The advantages of well-planned modular design of software are much of the same nature as those of modular hardware design. Independently written and assembled modules can be individually tested under simulated conditions and independently debugged. They can be updated and improved without materially affecting other modules; they can be "borrowed" from similar programs and "loaned out" to others. They can be viewed as "black boxes" with known terminal constraints and interface requirements and can be used accordingly. They can simplify the overall planning and design of the system.

There are disadvantages to an overmodularization. If the individual modules are too small, then linkage and control overhead can be costlier in software terms than the code savings/efficiency arising from the modularization. If there are too many modules, then some of the sought-after clarity disappears, particularly if the original problem is not really all that complex to begin with.

The nature of the assembler design problem is such that modularization is called for. We have chosen what appears to us to be a reasonable set of modules to maximize the advantages and minimize the disadvantages of modularity. We proceed to more clearly identify their functions below.

A top-level view of the modules

I/O module. This module clearly interfaces the assembler with the outside world, performing all input/output functions. For initial test purposes it could be written in a higher-level language like FORTRAN or Pascal, with subsequent conversion of selected portions into assembly language. As indicated in Section 10.1, we will not discuss I/O issues here. (The Exercises do probe somewhat more deeply into the module, however.)

Free-format decoder. This module takes the assembler source code, written according to free-format rules, and decodes it; that is, formats it into *label* (if present), *operation, operand,* and *remark* fields. It may save the free-format form of the line of code for listing purposes, but all other modules, for reasons of efficiency, use the decoded statement form.

Table entry/search module. This module handles all table operations: searching, sorting (if needed), and entry.

Location counter adjuster module. This module keeps track of the location counter during the assembly process. Based upon addressing modes used, instruction mnemonics, assembler directive types, default conventions, and so on, it adjusts the location counter to correctly allocate virtual memory and to properly define symbol values.

Error handler. This module is the source of diagnostic messages and the coordinator of all error conditions. It is called whenever an error is detected and, based upon the nature of the error, produces a message for the listing module and takes other appropriate actions.

Assembler directive processor module. This module is multifaceted and is, in reality, a collection of submodules, one for each assembler directive. Based upon the specific assembler directive encountered, the appropriate submodule is called to perform the required function. Different functions are required for an assembler directive, depending upon the pass the assembler is in.

Machine code generator module. This module generates the "traditional" object code of the assembler, that is, pairs of the form (virtual memory location, byte contents). To do this it uses the output of the expression evaluation and table search modules, along with the addressing modes and permanent symbol values.

Expression evaluation module. This module evaluates expressions found in the assembler source program, using symbol table searches if necessary. The exact rules concerning the legal forms of expressions and their evaluation are part of the syntax of the assembly language.

Listing module. This module, under the guidance of various listing control parameters, produces a listing of the source program and the object code, along with any error messages generated by the error handler module. Optionally symbol tables and so on may be listed, based upon these parameters.

10.4 Coordinating and Interfacing the Modules—I

We have specified, in general terms, a number of modules which obviously must form a part of the assembler, but aside from the very-high-level algorithm of Section 10.2, we have not discussed the exact method of linkage or coordination between these modules.

Toward that goal let us rewrite the high-level specification of the assembler passes in terms of module invocations:

Pass 1:

1. Set LC = 0.
2. Call I/O module to read a line of source code.
3. Call free-format decoder module to decode source line.
4. What type of statement is it?
    4.1. *.end*? Go to Pass 2.
    4.2 Assignment statement? Call expression evaluation module; Call table entry/search module to enter symbol and its value into symbol table, or call location counter adjuster if statement is of form *.=xxx*. Go to 2.
    4.3. Label present? Set it equal to LC value. Call table entry/search module to enter label and value into symbol table.
    4.4. Machine instruction? (Determine this by call to table entry/search module, searching permanent symbol tables.) Compute needed size in bytes, using default conventions if necessary and size information obtained from above call. Call location counter adjuster to do this. Go to 2.
    4.5. Assembler directive? (Determine this by call to table entry/search module, searching permanent symbol tables.) Call assembler directive processing module (which will call location counter adjuster) to compute needed size in bytes. Go to 2.
    4.6. Comment? Go to 2.
    4.7. Call error handler. Illegal statement type.

Pass 2:

1. Set LC = 0.
2. Place line of (unformatted) code into listing file. Look at formatted version of code.
3. What type of statement is it?
    3.1. *.end*? Go to *exit*.
    3.2. Assignment statement? If of type symbol =*xxx*, go to 4; otherwise Call Expression Evaluation Module; then Call Location Counter Adjuster Module.
    3.3. Machine instruction? (Determine this by call to table entry/search module searching permanent symbol tables.) Using information about operation code obtained from this call and operand values obtained from calls to the expression evaluation module and the table entry/ search module, generate machine code and place into listing file. The machine code generator module will handle this, as well as a call to the location counter adjuster module. Go to 4.
    3.4. Assembler directive? (Determine this by call to table entry/search module, searching permanent symbol tables.) Call assembler directive processing module, which will call location counter adjuster and, if necessary, generate object code. Place line of such object code into listing file. Go to 4.
    3.5. Comment? Go to 4.
    3.6. Call error handler. Illegal statement type.
4. Call listing generator to produce listing. Go to 2.

We have said that there may be a module called the executive module. What we have shown above is a specification, albeit informal, for the executive module. Consistent with our approach in the previous section, we will give a top-level description of it.

Executive module. This module directs all Pass 1 and Pass 2 activity of the assembler, calling the other modules in accordance with the plan above. It coordinates all such calls as well as error handling (see below). It does a minimal amount of "computation" itself.

What is missing in our discussion, in addition, is an informal calling net, that is, a graphical structure of "who" calls "whom." We give a preliminary one in Figure 10–1.

Clearly this is just a start; the problem one has in producing such a net is that the exact function and responsibilities of each module have not been specified. Our goal in Section 10.5 will be to do this; in particular, we must give special attention to the exact interplay between the expression evaluator, the table entry/search module, and the location counter adjuster.

Several thoughts on the philosophy of error handling are also needed at this time:

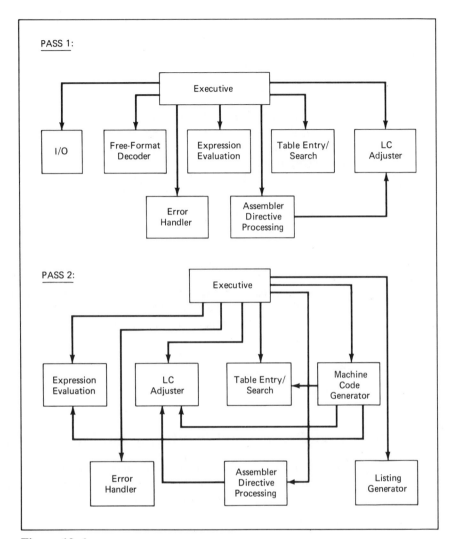

Figure 10–1.

The philosophy of error handling and the error handler. A modular system design readily allows for modular error handling under the control of the executive module. We can best describe such an approach as follows: Each module performs a specific, distinct function in the overall assembler design. Each module is thus capable of detecting error conditions as it performs its functions. The specific error conditions that a module detects are "spelled out" in the specification of that module—for example, the free-format decoder might detect an oversize label field.

The error handler module is not concerned with the error detection process per se. Rather, it only needs to know

1. In which module an error was detected,
2. What the error was ("message code"), and
3. What action to take, if any.

Let us pursue this line of thought a bit further.

A module will always return, as one of its call arguments, an error status flag, which will be used to indicate that an error was detected. We can agree by convention that this flag be set to 0 to indicate "normal module processing—no errors detected." Each distinct error can be assigned a unique code number which can easily be obtained if the flag is 1. These code numbers can be distinct for distinct modules as well. Thus items 1 and 2 above can readily be implemented by means of a numerical code. The error handler will contain, in its own storage area, a table for each module; corresponding to each error code can be a message in ASCII to be ultimately made available to the listing module. Further, corresponding to each error code can be an "action pointer" (item 3), which points to a routine for processing the action required. If the error is nonfatal, say a warning, the action routine might simply add a message line to the listing file so that it can be printed out in Pass 2. If it is fatal, necessitating a stopping of the assembly, such action can also be taken.

All of this is under control of the executive module. A diagram (top-level) of this strategy looks like Figure 10–2.

We discuss this, and all of the modules, further in the following section.

10.5   Coordinating and Interfacing the Modules—II

We propose to get at the heart of the module specification problem in this section by giving more detailed functional descriptions of each module. The general format of the description will be as follows:

Module name
Inputs
Outputs
General procedure
Exceptional conditions
Technical notes

After doing this for the modules we focus on the exact interplay of the modules by reexamining the executive routine and the calling net. Our description of the I/O module is minimal, as we have indicated earlier. We follow the same order of module specification as in Section 10.3, leaving the executive module for last. Note that our allocation of tasks to modules is somewhat arbitrary and our

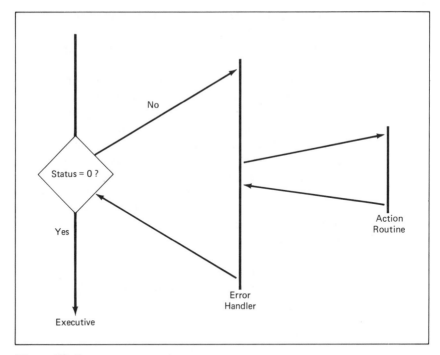

Figure 10–2.

discussion of error conditions still somewhat limited. The reason for the latter is that many details of the errors depend intimately on details of the language specification, a matter we have deferred discussing.

I/O module

Input: A record to read in from or write out to some device.

Output: In the case of reading, a "core image" of the record, accessible via a pointer; in the case of writing, the "core image" is output to the device.

General procedure: We leave this open here. For the purposes of initial assembler operation simple FORTRAN-like read/write statements will suffice.

Exceptional conditions, technical notes: For this module, we do not discuss these topics.

Free-format decoder

Input: An unformatted (free-format) source code line.

Output: A formatted source line containing the standard statement fields of VAX/MACRO in fixed positions easily accessible by pointers.

General procedure: Basically this procedure involves a search of the character strings comprising the line, looking for such characters as ":" or ";". We leave the detailed design of the module as an exercise for the reader.

Exceptional conditions: Typical of the types of errors to be encountered are "label field has too many symbols" or "illegal character found."

Technical notes: (1) This module might be termed a "lexical scanner" in compiler design. (2) In all probability the input is a pointer and the output four pointers, one for each type of statement field (possibly some are null). These output pointers will be used to reference this decoded statement in all subsequent processing operations in Pass 1 and Pass 2, saving unnecessary reformatting. Only in the listing generation process will the original form of the statement possibly be used. (3) In some sense, except for the I/O module, this module is the most independent of all the modules; if it were not there, the assembler could still run provided the user used a fixed format. Further, this module is truly a preprocessor to the assembler, as it only functions during Pass 1 and is not called by any module other than the executive module.

Table entry/search module

Inputs: A table name, a keyword, a flag, and possibly a value.

Output: Possibly a value.

General procedure: There are two modes of operation of this module—entry (flag = 0) and search (flag = 1). In search mode this operates as a search routine, looking for the keyword in the appropriate table and returning its found value. In entry mode, then, it is a table "builder," entering the keyword and its value into the specified table. The question of how keywords are stored (lexicographically, hashed, etc.) and how tables are searched (linear, binary, hashed, etc.) is discussed briefly below in the paragraph on technical notes.

Exceptional conditions: Any table operation which cannot be properly processed generates an error—for example, a request to search for a keyword that is not present, or to enter a (keyword, value) pair when the keyword has already been entered (multiply defined symbol).

Technical notes: (1) Many good references (e.g., Knuth [24]) exist on searching/entry/sorting techniques. The general rule of thumb is that if tables are small (say, 50 elements or so), then the linear search on an unordered table is more than adequate. For larger tables, particularly if they are *static* (like the machine operation table, e.g.,—see note 3, below), by ordering the table so that the most commonly used entries are first, a linear search can also often be used without serious penalty. (2) What kinds of tables are needed in an assembler? This will be addressed in note 3, below. But basically there are two types of tables, each having two general types of organization. There are *read-only* (static) tables, which are always searched and never modified during assembly time, and there are *read/write* (dynamic) tables. The two general types of organization are *fixed entry size* and *variable entry size*. The former is less efficient in the use of space [as the maximum (keyword, value) space must be allocated for each entry, irrespective of its actual size]. However, tables so organized are easy to sort and search. The latter is more efficient in its use of space, but some space must be allowed for linkage between successive, variable-size entries. "Pointer chasing," however, is quite time-consuming. For pedagogical reasons we will prefer to think of assemblers as having fixed-size entry tables. In Chapter 11, however, where we address the problems inherent to macroprocessing, we will discuss a variable-entry-size, directory-based approach to table organization. (3) At first glance the following tables are needed in our assembler's "data base":

Read-only tables

Machine operation table (machine instruction mnemonics, operation codes, etc.).
Assembler directive table (assembler directive mnemonics and their "action pointers").
Error message table.

Read/write tables

User-defined symbol table.

In the following section (Section 10.6) we discuss the data base in greater detail.

Location counter adjuster module

Inputs: The operation and operand fields of a source language statement and the old value of the location counter (for .=*xxx* a special input format is used) plus special information in the case of assembler directives.

Output: The new value of the location counter.

General procedure: The location counter adjuster must allocate the required amount of space for the instructions/assembler directives and, if the symbol "." appears in the context of "current LC value" = expression, must adjust the location counter value accordingly. In this latter case the expression evaluation module will be called. In the case of instructions, the mnemonic provides information on the data types of the operands; the addressing modes complement this to give an accounting of space required for the instruction. Default conventions must be employed, for example, in the case of relative mode addressing involving forward references. In the case of assembler directives, directive-specific interpretations must be provided to the location counter adjuster by the assembler directive module.

Exceptional conditions: We leave this somewhat vague here, but basically any situation which prevents unambiguous adjustment is an error. For example, a forward reference in a .=*xxx* statement or in the repetition factor of a *.byte* directive must generate an error code.

Technical notes: (1) We have been vague in our procedural description. Part of the problem stems from an exact allocation of responsibility issue. How much does the executive module do before calling the location counter adjuster? Does the executive module count the required number of bytes, reducing this module to a routine that essentially "increments" the LC, or is most of the work done within this module? For assembler directives the allocation of responsibility between this module and the assembler directive processor presents even more subtle problems. This "assignment of tasks" issue is one of the key ones in assembler design. We must make sure that every necessary function is performed once and only once. The Exercises explore this further. (2) Since "addressing modes" are critical to the proper operation of this module, and since these modes are indicated by distinct strings of characters, there could be an advantage to designing a somewhat more sophisticated free-format decoder that, during its scan, first checked to see if it had found an instruction mnemonic (by invoking the table entry/search module) and, finding this to be the case, continued its scan to pull off addressing modes. We would gain efficiency in the location counter adjustment problem, but add complexity and loss of "independence" to the free-format decoder. This type of trade-off is typical in modular software design.

Error handler module

Inputs: A module "code" and an error code.

Outputs: An error message and an "action" code (pointer).

General procedure: As indicated earlier (Section 10.4), the error handler module basically performs a table lookup function, involving the table entry/ search module. It produces a line of message for insertion into the listing file (see Section 10.6 for a discussion of the data base) and sends back an action code (pointer) to the executive module, which can then take appropriate action.

Exceptional conditions: These only occur if an illegal message code or error code is encountered.

Technical note: There is no real need, logically, for this module in that it could be part of the table entry/search module. But from the point of view of modular design it is useful to view the error handler as a distinct module and the table entry/search module as a kind of utility.

Assembler directive processor module

Inputs: The operation and operand fields of an assembler directive and a *pass* flag (1 or 2).

Output: For Pass 1 there is no direct output, just a location counter adjustment. For Pass 2, depending on the directive, object code may be generated and placed into the object file.

General procedure: There are really several "modules" contained with this single module, based upon the pass we are in and the type of assembler directive. Some directives allocate and possibly initialize portions of virtual memory; others merely affect the listing, for example. Some in VAX/MACRO are not related to the intrinsic features of the language. Thus in this paragraph we will merely comment as follows. Associated with each directive in the assembler directive table is an "action pointer" to a procedure to process it. There may be two such pointers, one for each pass. The pointers are followed and modules such as the location counter adjuster may be called. A special part of the assembler directive processor will be the object code generator which processes directives such as *.word* or *.ascii*.

Exceptional conditions: Again there are too many to enumerate, but typical ones would be a value too large for a *.byte* directive or a missing delimiter in an *.ascii* directive.

Technical notes: (1) In the process of writing this module we may logically view it as consisting of two parts—a Pass 1 processor and a Pass 2 processor. The only "Pass 1" directives are those that affect the location counter value; the action pointers for all of the other assembler directives may be viewed as being "*null*" for the Pass 1 part. All directives must be processed in Pass 2. (2) As indicated in the "Technical notes" portion of the "Location counter adjuster module," there is a delicate allocation of responsibilities to be performed among the various modules. For example, if the line

```
.byte 50[30]
```

appears, does the executive module, the location counter adjuster, or the assembler directive processor do the multiplication by 30? Our own "gut feeling" is that the assembler directive processor "passes" a 1 (for *byte*) and the 30 to the location counter adjuster, which in effect completes the computation. But details have to be resolved by the assembler designer.

Machine code generator module

Inputs: The operation and operand fields of a machine code instruction.

Output: Object code, that is, pairs of the form (location, byte contents) corresponding to the machine code for the instruction.

General procedure: The operation of the module is fairly clear in general terms. Using the table entry/search module the operation code for the mnemonic can be obtained, as well as default information about the instruction operands (see section 10.6 for a more in-depth discussion of the data base). For each operand, using, where needed, calls to the expression evaluation module or table entry/ search module, the appropriate machine code can be generated. It can also be placed in the listing file.

Exceptional conditions: Typical of conditions here are inappropriate addressing modes for the instruction type or operands that, as forward references, were allocated default space and turn out to have values that are too large to "fit" into the allocated space.

Technical notes: (1) Some serious thought has to be given to the role, if any, that instruction operand access and data types play in the machine code generation process. We leave this to the Exercises. (2) Some subtle interplay issues arise here between this module and the expression evaluation and table entry/search modules. How is a single user-defined symbol to be evaluated? Should all operands be directly passed to the expression evaluator, even if the "expression" is just a symbol? (3) This module will probably contain some base conversion utility procedures for going from the default notation of decimal into hexadecimal or binary.

Expression evaluation module

Input: An expression made up of operands and operations.

Output: The value of the expression.

General procedure: In many systems this would be considered to be a *utility* module. The concept of an expression is well defined; so is the concept of the value of an expression. This module, through calls to the table entry/search module (for obtaining the values of user-defined symbols), performs such evaluation following the precedence and syntax rules of VAX/MACRO.

Exceptional conditions: There are, in general, two types of exceptional conditions: "syntactic" and "semantic." In the former category the form of the expression is illegal—for example, unmatched angle brackets or an illegal character. In the latter case either a symbol is undefined or the obtained value is too large (overflow).

Technical notes: (1) Some of the syntax checking could be done in the free-format decoder module—for example, illegal operators or unbalanced brackets. We come back again to this issue of the "division of labor"—this can be done at the price of a more complex, less independent free-format decoder. (2) The exact procedure for evaluating expressions is merely an implementation of the definitions given in the *VAX-11 MACRO Language Reference Manual* [18].

Listing module

Input: The listing file and a table of control parameters.

Output: A modified listing file.

General procedure: We will say little about this module, which is principally controlled by parameter values set by assembler directives (or by default values). A "master" listing file is kept during the assembly process, containing the complete object code in ASCII and tables of symbols, cross-references, and so on. The modified listing file is an (abridged) version of this file, based upon user requests through the use of the assembler directives. Directives such as *.title* may actually add to this file.

Exceptional conditions: It is hard to imagine any errors that would explicitly be detected by this module—errors in listing specifications would be caught by the assembler directive processor module, errors in characters and so on by the I/O module.

Technical notes: (1) The master file has a default size and is reserved in a working storage area of the listing module. The listing probably contains the free-format version of the source code or, optionally, the decoded, formatted version. (2) The module will add line numbers, and the listing file, as modified, will contain appropriate error messages. It is reasonable to assume that the line numbers are attached to statements during the free-format decoding phase of Pass 1 and thereafter carried around with all processing of the statement. The error handler, when it creates an error message, can attach this line number, and the listing module will do the final "synthesis" to make sure that the line numbers of the error message and the listing coincide.

10.6 The Data Base for the Assembler

In this brief section we wish to examine the various data structures we have discussed in greater detail. We begin with the machine operation table, the discussion of which sets the tone for this entire section.

Machine operation table

Type: Static.

Purpose: To record, for each machine mnemonic in the source language, information such as the number (operation) code, the number of arguments, the argument data types, and the allowable argument addressing modes. This intrinsic information forms the "value" of the instruction mnemonic, the "keyword."

Organization: Fixed block size; probably lexicographically ordered to facilitate a rapid binary search, although it could be ordered according to the most commonly encountered mnemonics, making a simpler linear search feasible.

Size: If there are N machine mnemonics and the maximum information needed per mnemonic is W bytes, then this table is NW bytes in length.

Technical notes: (1) The exact nature of what should be stored within this table is left somewhat vague here, but intuitively it may be viewed as analogous to the appendices of the language reference manuals. (2) From an implementation point of view, we make the following remark: Were we writing the assembler in VAX/MACRO, we would create this table via a sequence of *.ascii* and *.byte* directives to record alphanumeric and binary contents, respectively.

Assembler directive table

Type: Static.

Purpose: To provide, for each assembler-directive mnemonic in the source language, a pair of pointers, one for use in Pass 1 processing, one for use in Pass 2 processing. The pointers, which we have termed "action pointers," lead to directive-specific procedures for processing the directives in the given pass of the assembler. Pointers are null if the directive needs no processing in a given pass (e.g., a listing control directive is Pass 1).

Organization: Fixed block size. Lexicographically ordered for binary search, or linearly searched with an ordering favoring most commonly used directives.

Size: NW, where *N* is the number of directives, and *W* is the number of bytes needed to store the two action pointers.

Technical notes: (1) The null pointer can be a special address, or alternatively a null/nonnull flag could be allocated. (2) As indicated in our discussion in the previous section, we may view this table as, in reality, being two tables, one for Pass 1 and one for Pass 2.

Error message table

Type: Static.

Purpose: As discussed earlier, this table is the respository of error messages and corresponding "action pointers."

Organization: Fixed block size. Since the error code may be viewed as an integer, this table need only be ordered by code number and simple indexing suffices to search it or to obtain a given entry.

Size: NW, where *N* is the number of codes and *W* is the number of bytes needed to store the error messages and the "action pointers."

Technical notes: (1) The "action pointer" here is probably just a code itself indicating distinct actions—for example, stop assembly, append "*warning*" to the message, and send to the listing file, and so on. (2) As indicated above, because the error codes are numerical the table is effectively hash-addressed and a single index operation is sufficient to access any message/action code.

The last two data structures contained in this discussion are, unlike the first three, dynamic tables, whose contents depend upon the specific source program being assembled. The allocation of space for these tables may be viewed as fixed; so "dynamic" refers to the contents of the table, as well as its size in terms of data entered.

User-defined symbol table

Type: Dynamic.

Purpose: To record the names and values of all user-defined symbols in the source language program.

Organization: Fixed block size. Unless source program sections are extremely large, the user-defined symbol table will be of a limited size that will probably permit a linear search to work efficiently. Ordering a dynamic table to allow binary searching/entry is very time-consuming.

Size: The working size (as opposed to the allocated size) is proportional to the number of user-defined symbols. We may assume that each value is a longword of data.

Technical note: A legitimate case may be made for a variable entry size here. After all, machine mnemonics/assembler directives are all roughly 2–4 characters long, whereas symbol names can vary from 1 to 10 or so characters in length, depending on the specific assembly language. However, as indicated earlier, we take the fixed-block approach in this chapter. Variable block size, and its incumbent extra overhead, are only justified, in our minds, when a significant space savings is foreseen. We explore this in Chapter 11 in the context of macro-processing.

Listing file

Type: Dynamic.

Purpose: To contain ASCII data permitting a listing/display of the source and object program, cross-references, error messages, symbol definitions, and so forth.

Organization: We view this file as record-organized, using, in the case of a line printer–based listing, around 132 characters (bytes) per record.

Size: The working size is a function of the number of source lines, the number of error messages, and so on.

Technical note: Again we distinguish between the master listing file (the one being discussed here) and the "seen" listing file produced by the listing module under control of the various listing-oriented assembler directives. The reader is referred to the Section 10.5.

10.7 The Calling Net Revisited

What we do in this section may be viewed as an attempted synthesis of our discussions to date. In particular, we wish to add to our module specifications of Section 10.5 two more entries:

Modules called
Modules called by

After doing this we will attempt to redraw the calling net presented in Section 10.4 to "incorporate" these entries. We conclude this section with a renewed look at the executive module, leaving many details to the reader in the Exercises.

Table of calls

We can streamline the "call information" presentation by means of the table in Figure 10–3. It is constructed on the basis of the information contained in the previous sections of this chapter. Note that the executive module, as the highest-level routine, is not called by any other module. A checkmark in row *i*, column *j* means that module *i calls* module *j*. We add the following remarks:

1. The low-level (utility) modules are modules that call no other modules:

I/O
Free-format decoder

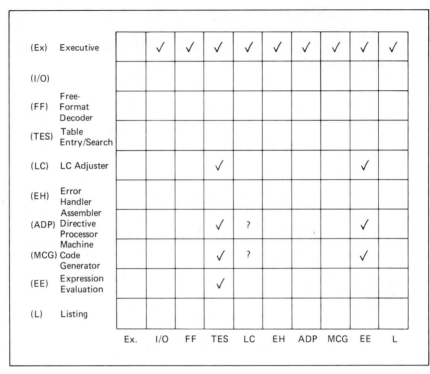

Figure 10–3.

Table entry/search
Listing generator
Error handler

Identifying these modules is important in modular design. These can be easily tested, under simulation conditions, as separate units. They can easily be replaced by more sophisticated, specialized units in future versions of the assembler.

2. The question marks ("?") reflect the "assignment of responsibility" issues we encountered in Section 10.5. The reader is urged to review those issues in the context of this table.

Calling net

The redrawn calling net of Figure 10–1 is given in Figure 10–4. We do not separate the passes here. This symbolic structure is of maximum use only when other "resources" are available, such as the top-level descriptions of Sections 10.5 and 10.6. This is a "control flow" calling net, not a "data flow" net. The latter involves answering the questions of how data are passed between modules and which modules access which parts of the data base. This is left as an exercise for the reader.

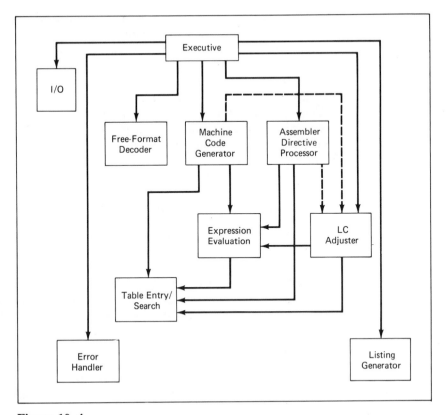

Figure 10–4.

Notice that there is a hierarchial structure here which is not as evident in the net of Section 10.4. Such a structure is an essential part of the modular design process.

To complete the developments we add a description of the executive module in a fashion analogous to other module descriptions.

Executive module

   Inputs: A source program in VAX/MACRO.
   Outputs: Object code, including a listing, if requested.
   General procedure: The general procedure has been discussed several times. Two passes are made through the source program: the goal of the first pass is to define user-defined symbols; the goal of the second is, in effect, to do everything else. A modular structure of specialized procedures is invoked to allow this to be done. All errors are processed through the executive module, which, upon receiving indications of errors at lower-level modules, calls an error handler module.

Exceptional conditions: Any source program containing one or more features not permitting complete assembly clearly cannot be considered "successful."

Technical notes: (1) We envision this routine as essentially a series of procedure calls to the other modules, with some minimal decision-making ability in it, based upon the results of the calls. (2) What needs to be further defined are the myriad small data structures (addresses, counters, flags, etc.) needed to effect argument passage and argument evaluation. (3) Who debugs the assembler itself? One advantage of the structured, hierarchical assembler executive is that during assembler development simple trace routines can be used to isolate problems and improve performance.

10.8   Putting the Pieces Together: A Summary

Let us stand back and assess what we have done thus far in this chapter. We have:

1. Discussed the general issues involved in writing an assembler.
2. Proposed and discussed in some detail a modular design structure for an assembler and the interrelation between the parts of this structure.
3. Described the data structures (data base) needed to effect the program functioning of the modules.

What have we *not done*? We have not:

1. Actually written any code. This has not been our objective.
2. Discussed the modular structure in sufficient detail to allow an immediate "transition" into working code.
3. Addressed every single issue/detail in writing an assembler.

What, then, have we attempted to do? As indicated in the introduction to this chapter, we have tried to uncover critical issues for the reader and to allow the reader to reconcile them with what he or she has learned about the use of VAX/MACRO.

The reader has learned, in Part I of this book, *how* to use the VAX/MACRO language. He or she has learned the various syntax rules, instructions, directives, addressing modes, and so on. What we seek to achieve in Part II is to understand what the assembler must do to process each type of feature in the language. We have not answered these questions completely, but with the help of the Exercises we feel we have proposed the proper framework in which to address them.

What would the reader have to do if, at this point, he or she wanted to *write* the assembler? Let us identify the important steps:

1. Make a checklist of every assembly language feature that has to be handled. Certify that it is handled by exactly one module.
2. Specify the module functions in much greater detail (e.g., a flowchart or pseudo-code). Pay particular attention to exceptional conditions and where they occur.

3. Do an intensive study of interfacing—which parameters are passed, and how they are accessed. Which data areas are local to a module, and which are common to all modules?

4. Firm up the data base. What are the table sizes and organizations? Are the static tables ordered? If so, how?

5. Select a language in which to write each module. Reexamine steps 1–4 in the context of the chosen language.

6. Be careful and heavily document the code for each module.

7. Develop test procedures for each module to be unit-tested, under simulated input conditions.

8. Develop a module integration plan at the software level.

9. Properly estimate the completion time for each module. Experienced programmers often take their initial "worst case" estimates and double them or triple them to arrive at a reasonable estimate.

10. Develop test procedures for the integrated system that, in theory, test all of the features of the assembler and all of the logical pathways in the code.

Where we go from here

Recall that we have been involved in this chapter with intrinsic features of the assembler. We introduce in the following chapter the concept of macros and the related processing required. The issues involved in processing macros are interesting and present different types of data structures and modularization. Following this we introduce the problem of linker design and global symbols, completing our discussion of "what makes VAX/MACRO work?"

Exercises

Section 10.1

1. a. Read through the *VAX/MACRO Language Reference Manual* [18], several times if necessary.
   b. Mark all features according to whether you feel that they are intrinsic (I), global (G), or macro-related (M).

Section 10.2

2. a. Discuss the various *default* conventions in intrinsic VAX/MACRO. Why are they needed?
   b. Discuss the various restrictions on *forward references* that you see. Why should there be any in a two-pass assembler? Under what conditions will a single-pass assembler be possible? Will N passes ($N > 2$) be necessary if certain restrictions on forward references are removed?
   c. Divide the assembler directives into the following categories: listing-related, data generation, location counter control, other. For each directive write a short sentence describing what it does and in which pass it should be done.

3. The general assembler design proposed here could be called "deferred" in that the minimum amount of work possible is done in Pass 1; the maximum in Pass 2. Propose

the counterpart to this, wherein Pass 2 does as little as possible. Such assemblers are often misnamed "single-pass" assemblers.

4. Draw a flowchart for the top-level assembler algorithm given here. Before reading Section 10.3 try to identify modular functions intrinsic to the flowchart.

Section 10.3

5. (The I/O module.) Try to propose the structure of the I/O module in more detail. In particular, consider such issues as the physical device, the data organization (blocked, character, binary), and the form of access.

6. (The free-format decoder.) What are the format rules of VAX/MACRO? What are the implications, according to these rules, of missing fields, and so on?

7. We have described one modular decomposition. Can you suggest others for the assembler? (General discussion.)

8. This exercise proposes a simple mathematical model of the modularization process. Suppose that program P has k lines with execution time $(alpha)*(k**n)$ and "debug time" $(beta)*(k**n)$. Suppose that P is divided into $M0$ modules of $(k/M0)$ lines each with execution and debug times of $(alpha)*(k/M0**n)$ and $(beta)*(k/M0**n)$, respectively. Suppose finally that the linkage overhead for $M0$ modules is $(gamma*M0)$. Under what conditions will modularization save time? That is, will the total time for debugging, executing, and linking be less than $(alpha)*(k**n) + (beta)*(k**n)$? When does modularization not pay, from the time point of view?

Section 10.4

9. Using your favorite high-level language, "write" the executive module of Section 10.4 as a sequence of procedure calls and "decisions." (Since we have only informally specified the "parameters" of various modules, this "writing" is more of a "sketch.")

10. Try to identify five errors for each module, assign error "codes" and messages, and suggest appropriate "actions."

11. The calling net is a "control flow" net; that is, it shows "who *calls* whom." Can you draw a "data flow" net which shows how data are passed? For example, the machine code generator passes object code to the listing module (through the executive module, possibly).

Section 10.5

12. We can focus on some of the issues of the free-format decoder by writing one ourselves for a simpler format. Suppose we say that there are no continuation lines, and no blank lines, and that therefore a statement must fit into exactly one line. Let us further assume that the statement is at most 80 characters, not counting the terminating carriage return. Let us also restrict the label field to between 1 and 7 characters and the character set of the label field to be A–Z, 0–9 except for the last character, which is a ":". All other rules of VAX/MACRO apply. Write a free-format decoder (in VAX/MACRO or any other language) to implement this design.

13. This exercise deals with a simple mathematical model of table entry/search issues.
    a. Assume that we have a table of N elements and that if linearly searched we find what we are looking for in $N/2$ operations at a cost of beta seconds per operation. For a binary search assume that we need $\log_2 N$ operations at a cost of alpha > beta seconds per operation. If alpha = $k*$beta, for what value of N does a binary search pay? (Assume $N >= 2$.)
    b. Assume that the elements of a table can range from $N0$ to $M0$ in size, $N0 <= M0$. Assume that for a fixed block size organization, $M0$ bytes per block, a linear search

takes alpha seconds per block. If the table has N blocks, how much space is needed? How much time to conclude an element is not there? What is the time–storage product? Repeat this analysis for a variable block size, adding two elements per block for linkage and assuming a time of beta > alpha and a block size of ($N0$ + $M0$)/2. Under what conditions is the variable-block-size model justified?

14. Give size estimates for the tables discussed under "Table entry/search module" using your actual knowledge about VAX/MACRO.

15. Write a description of what must be done to adjust the location counter during assembly to convince yourself of the nature of the problems involved. Use actual examples, for this purpose, from the beginning of the text (Part I). Comment in particular on the role of the following features of VAX/MACRO in the location counter adjuster design: variable instruction size, addressing modes, and defaults.

16. (The assignment of tasks.) We have alluded throughout this section to the proper division of labor. Propose a model for the location counter adjuster which allows it to do the maximum amount of "relevant" work. Using this model, describe the typical scenario encountered for machine instructions and for assembler directives. Now propose a model for this module which lets it do the minimal amount of work (perhaps no more than a simple "incrementation"). Repeat the above scenario description. Which modules are doing the work that the more complex location counter adjuster did?

17. Our approach to error handling might be described as "centralized." An alternative approach is to have distributed error handling in which each routine, upon finding an error, generates its own messages, actions, and so on. What are the advantages/disadvantages of this approach vis-à-vis the centralized approach? Will an error handler module still be needed?

18. We have attempted to create modules that fairly evenly divide the work. Propose a mathematical model of modularization which takes into account the number of modules, the size of the modules, and the interfacing/coordinating problem (a simple model) that justifies numerically the fact that we write an assembler modularly but write a sorting routine, for example, as a single unit. (See exercise 8.)

19. (Action pointers and assembler directives.) Suppose, for the sake of this exercise, that VAX/MACRO only has the following assembler directives:

```
.show      .ascii    .byte
.nshow     .ascic    .word
.default   .ascid    .long
.end       .asciz    .address
.blka
.blkb
.blkl
.blkw
```

Try to define the "action routines" needed to process them. An informal English-language description will suffice. Be particularly sensitive to the "allocation of responsibilities" issue, with respect to related modules. (See also exercise 16.)

20. Give an algorithmic description of the machine code generator module. In particular, focus on the role that operand access/data types may play and on the need for automatic recognition of addressing modes and permanent symbols.

21. (See also exercise 18.) The modular structure introduced here may have some modules that themselves need to be decomposed. A logical candidate for this is the machine code generator module. Typical subfunctions are base conversion, addressing mode recognition (the location counter adjuster might profit from such a module also), object

code creator, and so on. Propose such a decomposition and specify the function of each module.

22. Sketch a procedure for doing expression evaluation according to the syntax of VAX/MACRO, using the rules for order of evaluation.

23. Using the *VAX/MACRO Language Reference Manual* [18], attempt to define the various "listing options." Using these definitions, propose a design for the listing module. Use for the "master" listing file any organization which seems reasonable.

Section 10.6

24. Try to specify the exact contents of the machine operation table. Only include information that is needed during assembly. Attempt to propose a format that considers both efficiency in time to access/process and storage space.

25. Repeat exercise 24 for the assembler directive table.

26. Tables such as the error message table are typically stored in ASCII. Other tables are binary. What are the issues involved in deciding as to the format of a table, as opposed to the contents? What can you say about the overhead of converting from one representation to another?

Section 10.7

27. (See also exercises 4 and 9) Let us again attempt to specify the executive module in flowchart form. With our much greater state of knowledge we should be able to go from this flowchart to a high-level implementation that not only interfaces with the modules but clearly defines "global" items of data. What are some of these?

28. We have described a single executive structure. How would a two-executive structure (one for each pass) work? What would be its advantages? Its disadvantages? Are any other structures of modular design possible for an assembler?

Chapter 11

Macroprocessor Design Issues

11.1   Introduction

Let us turn to, in this chapter, the macroprocessing aspects of VAX/MACRO. We will again keep our discussion fairly general and representative of macroprocessing issues in the large—the Exercises will explore the VAX/MACRO macro features in greater detail.

We will assume that the reader has used a macro facility before, be it that of VAX/MACRO or that of a similar macroassembler. Such facilities permit the user to extend the "instruction set" of the assembly language in a flexible, orderly fashion by allowing the macro user to (1) define macros; (2) invoke, or call, macros; and (3) nest macro calls (and definitions) to allow a "recursive" growth in the process of language extensibility.

In a certain sense macroprocessing is a specialized form of text editing. We adopt this philosophy here. In particular, we view the macroprocessor as a preprocessor to the assembler which transforms source code containing macro features into the "intrinsic," "pure" source code of Chapter 10.

As in the preceding chapter, we do not produce working code, but we do attempt to identify critical modular design issues.

11.2   The Basic Features of Macroprocessors

In this section we summarize, in general terms, the basic features of macroprocessors. The reader may want to view this development as a kind of overview of the VAX/MACRO macro facilities, devoid of syntactical details. We are seeking to develop some terminology here, as well as some notation, and some underlying concepts, to better prepare for our modular design that follows.

Macro definitions

The typical mechanism for defining macros in a macroprocessor is through the use of two specialized assembler directives, usually called *macro* and *endm*. Logically they may be viewed as equivalent to "(" and ")" in that they serve to bracket the "prototypical" structure of the macro. What we mean by "prototypical" is that the macro definition is usually parameterized; the parameter values are specified during the call to the macro. Thus the definition is but the basic structure of the macro, a kind of generic form of the macro.

The usual appearance of a macro definition is as follows:

$$.macro \quad name, \ P_1, \ ..., \ P_k$$
$$.$$
$$. \qquad (body \ of \ macro)$$
$$.$$
$$.endm \quad name$$

where *name* is the macro name and $P_1, \ ..., \ P_k$ are the macro parameter specifications. Each P_J is of the form

$$symbol \quad or \quad symbol = default \ value$$

The default value may be viewed as being present in the first type of specification, with its value being that of the null string. (We view, recalling our earlier remarks above, all macro operations as essentially being string processing operations.)

For ease of discussion below we introduce the following notation: the symbol part of P_J will be denoted by $S\ (P_J)$, and is called the Jth parameter of the macro.

The body of the macro consists of lines of text. The character set of the macroassembler is divided, for the purpose of macroprocessing, into two classes: nondelimiting characters and delimiting characters. Usually all alphanumeric characters are considered as nondelimiting, and typical delimiters are: " ", ", ", "*tab*", etc. We say that the parameter $S\ (P_J)$ "occurs" in line L of the macro body if L contains a substring of the form $...\ CS\ (P_J)D\ ...$, where C and D are delimiting characters. Clearly, to allow a consistent, unambiguous application of these concepts, all symbols serving as parameter names consist of only nondelimiting characters. Note that one consequence of this rather obvious restriction is that if both $S(P_J)$ and $S(P_m)$ occur in line L, then they occur as distinct substrings of L, and not as overlapping parts of some single substring of L.

To allow the macroprocessor to "find" the *endm* statement that terminates the macro definition, a further restriction is usually placed upon the contents of the macro body—it cannot contain, in any line, the string *endm*. For similar reasons, that will become apparent later when we discuss recursive macro constructions, the string *macro* is not permitted either.

(The last two statements are not quite true when "nested" macro definitions are allowed. All internal *macro* strings must be balanced by matching *endm* strings. We defer discussion of these issues until Section 11.5.)

Macro calls

A call to the macro *name* is a statement outside the definition of *name* whose operation field, interpreted in the standard format context of the macroprocessor, is *name* and whose operand field is a string "S" of one of the two general forms described below.

Before giving this description we want to say a few words about the issue of "format." As we know from our use of assembly language, any statement is regarded as containing up to four distinct fields—label, operation, operand, and remarks. Usually, in assembly language there is a freedom of formatting, allowing flexibility in the placement of these fields within the assembly language statement. Most macroprocessors are intimately integrated with the assemblers that they are preprocessors to. Thus macro call statements inherit the field definitions of the assembler. We take this philosophy here. Let us make this more explicit.

The input to the macroprocessor is a source program containing macro definitions and macro calls as well as plain, ordinary, "pure" assembly language statements. The output is a "pure" (intrinsic) assembly language program that is stripped of macro definitions and in which all macro calls in the input program have been expanded. All statements in the input source program to the macroprocessor inherit the field definitions of the assembler except the statements comprising the macro body, which are just viewed as character strings. (As indicated earlier, we will amend this latter comment when we discuss recursion in Section 11.5.)

Thus macro calls are those source statements whose operand fields correspond to the names of defined macros. In theory, one can, by defining a macro to have the same name as that of a standard machine mnemonic, render that mnemonic nonexistent in its original, manufacture-intended sense. The Exercises deal with this problem.

Returning to our comments at the beginning of this section, there are two general formats for the operand field of a macro call. The purpose of this string "S" is to define, for each parameter $S(P_J)$ of the macro definition, a "call string" that will serve to replace all occurences of $S(P_J)$ in the body of the macro.

Thus "S" must contain, for each J, either a string to substitute for $S(P_J)$ or a request to use, instead, the default value for $S(P_J)$ specified in the definition of the macro. One way of doing this is called positional argument specification. To specify positionally a substitution string or a request for default use for each $S(P_J)$ we write "S" in the form below:

$$q_1, q_2, \ldots, q_m$$

where the following apply:

1. m is less than or equal to k.
2. If m = k, then some of the q_J can be null, in which case two or more consecutive commas appear in "S". If m is less than k, then, furthermore, $q_{m+1}, ..., q_k$ are regarded as being null.
3. All nonnull q_J are subject to certain syntax restrictions.
4. The values to be substituted for the symbols $S(P_J)$ are determined as follows: if q_J is null, then the default value for $S(P_J)$ as specified in the macro definition is to be used. If q_J is nonnull, then this nonnull value is to be used.
5. In particular, then, if q_J is null and so is the default value for $S(P_J)$, then the null string will replace all occurrences of $S(P_J)$ in the macro body.

As complex as the above rules sound, they are precisely the ones that we "intuitively" use for positional macro calling. Note that, for obvious reasons, arguments containing commas are not allowed, unless the commas can somehow be suitably distinguished from real, separating commas.

The other general mechanism for specifying macro arguments in a macro call is usually called keyword argument specification. This is a particularly useful form of specification when the macro contains many arguments, but most often they tend to take default values. In keyword specification we only specify the call values for the arguments that are not to be defaulted. The general form of the call string is

$$S(P_{i1}) = q_1, ..., S(P_{in}) = q_n$$

where the order of $i1, ..., in$ is irrelevant (obviously the values $i1, ..., in$ are distinct and each is less than or equal to k) and the q_J are either nonnull (obeying some syntactical restriction) or null.

11.3 Macroprocessor Design Issues: General

A macroprocessor has two basic functions to perform: process (record) definitions and expand calls. The call expansion function may be divided into two subfunctions: recognizing macro calls and producing call expansions via parameter substitution. We will assume in the discussion below that no recursive definition/call facility is present. We will address the issue of recursion in macroprocessors in Section 11.5, as indicated earlier.

We give an informal summary of the basic design questions for macroprocessors below. The reader should note that many of these questions arose, in a somewhat different context, in the case of assembler design.

1. Clearly macro definitions (macro bodies) must be saved in some kind of table. Call this table the macro definitions table (MDT). Should this table be of

fixed block size? Should it be maintained in some kind of order so as to facilitate searches? How, exactly, should the macro definitions be stored?

2. How are searches for the parameters in macro bodies to be handled? What about argument substitution and default values?

3. What about error handling? What kinds of errors can arise? How are they to be detected? How about changes in statement length due to argument substitution? Can this cause format problems for the assembler?

Clearly, before any software development can proceed, we must address all of these issues and more. Let us begin here by introducing a design philosophy that is, on the surface, radically different than the one used for assemblers: a single-pass macroprocessor.

Let us try to review the reasons for two-pass design in assemblers and let us see whether the same reasons are compelling in macroprocessor design. Single-pass design means, for all practical purposes, that forward references to as yet unde-fined constructs are not permitted. This absence is, in practice, far too restrictive in assembly language programming.

On the contrary, in the case of macroprocessor design, the restriction is not an unreasonable one at all. Requiring that macros not be called until they have been defined is, in fact, a reasonable restriction to have in a macroprocessor. Macro libraries or user-created files of macro definitions can be placed at the beginning of any macroassembly program without seriously impeding the creative use of macrodefinitions and calls. The same cannot be said in general with regard to forward symbolic references in assembly language programming. Requiring a user to only address symbolically statements that are before a program statement has an impact upon the structure of the code.

Thus accepting that one-pass macroprocessing is reasonable, what are the phases of macroprocessor design?

1. Macro definitions are recognized by their delimiting sets of *.macro* and *.endm* directives. They are entered, in a form to be detailed below, into a master directory of macro definitions, which we have termed the macro definitions table.

2. As discussed earlier, outside macro definitions, the macroprocessor uses the same formatting/fields conventions as does the assembler. Thus whenever an operation field is encountered, it is checked against all existing macro names. If no match is found, then the operation field is not viewed as a macro call. Note that a call to a macro defined later in the macroassembler source program (a forward reference) is not treated as a macro call. In all probability the assembler will treat it as a undefined operation field.

3. The definitions, when "entered," are removed from the macro source file. The calls, too, are replaced by their expansions. Thus, the assembler receives "pure" source code. When we say "removed" we are speaking figuratively. In all likelihood the original macroprocessor input source file is retained for listing/

debugging purposes. A "copy file" is created as the output file. It is passed on to the assembler. All nonmacro calls are placed directly onto the copy file, macrodefinitions are not, and, while macro calls are not placed in the copy file either, their expansions are.

Design issues for macroprocessors

Based upon our discussions to date we can identify a modular structure in macroprocessing. Much as was the case in the preceding chapter, the definitions and choice of these modules is somewhat arbitrary. This modular structure is, however, based upon an attempt to capture the intuitively distinct, identifiable functions of the macroprocessor:

Definition entry module
Call recognition module
Argument list preparer module
Text generation module
Error handler
I/O module

We will approach the specification of these modules in much the same way that we did in Chapter 10. We will assume, for the time being, that there are no recursive call/definition capabilities as previously mentioned.

Definition entry module. This module enters into a directory of macro definitions the body of the macro. In making this entry it is usually most efficient to search for the parameters of the macro upon entry—this allows them to be specially marked and avoids repetitive searches for them upon macro expansion during call processing (e.g., see Donovan 1969 [25]).

Call recognition module. This module performs a search of the macro definitions table to see whether or not the operation field of a statement is indeed a macro call.

Argument list preparer module. This module "prepares" the list of macro call arguments, whether they be user-specified or default values, and whether the specification be positional or keyword.

Text generation module. This module is the heart of the macroprocessor. During the processing of a macro call it goes through the body of the macro definition line by line replacing macro parameters with their "call values" as prepared by the argument list preparer. This module performs a specialized form of text editing.

Error handler. As in the assembler, this module is the "clearinghouse" for all error message and related actions.

I/O module. We do not discuss this module in any detail. It in part interfaces the macroprocessor output with the assembler input. It may also produce a listing of the macro expansions, although usually all listings are handled by the assembler.

Some further comments on text generation

Because of the complex nature of text expansion and because of the intimate link between the macro processor and the assembler, we wish to engage in a brief, "esoteric" discussion of the macroprocessor text generation concept.

Each line "L" of a macro definition's body has two "states," L0 and L1. L0 is the state of line L as stored in the macro definitions table, that is, with specially delimited parameters but with no "final argument substitution done." L1 is the state of L after arguments have replaced the parameters during the processing of a macro call. It is L1 that the assembler sees and, except in the context of the recursion issues we will discuss in Section 11.5, the format of L1 is of no interest to the macroprocessor. In particular, then, we regard the generation of meaningless code, violating assembler syntax rules, as a problem external to the macroprocessing function. Such "code" will be caught by the assembler (for example, by the free-format decoder).

11.4   A More Detailed Look at Modules and Data Base

Let us mimic the approach to module specification seen in the preceding chapter. For each module we will describe the inputs, outputs, general procedure, exceptional conditions, and the key technical points. We will also briefly describe the executive module and the data base issues.

Definition entry module

Inputs: The source statements comprising the definition of a macro, including the *.macro* and the *.endm* statements.

Outputs: An updated macro definitions directory.

General procedure: This module updates the master directory of macro definitions. The macro name, parameter list, and macro body are recorded in the directory.

Exceptional conditions: Typical of the types of errors that this module may detect are "multiply defined" macros (if we wish to regard this as an error—some systems permit the redefinition of a macro), excessive length of body, illegal syntax in the *.macro* statement, and so forth.

Technical notes: (1) Because of the extreme variability of the size of macro definitions, a variable-block-size table is most appropriate. Accompanying this table will be a "directory" that is of fixed block size and that allows rapid linear searching of macro definitions. (2) As indicated earlier, macro parameters can be specially marked during entry to avoid repetitive searches for them during call expansion. Usually a non-user-allowed character, delimiting the parameter on both sides, will suffice here. (3) This module is called into action in the following context. A *.macro* statement is seen in the source by the executive module. This statement and all ensuing source statements up to and including the *.endm* statement are copied into a special file and then passed to the definition entry module for entry.

Call recognition module

Input: The operation field of a source statement in the macroassembly language.

Output: A flag (*yes* if it is a macro call; *no* if it is not) and a pointer to the body of the macro if it is a call.

General procedure: The macro definitions table is searched for the name in the operand field. If it is found, then a macro call has occurred. The "directory" points to the stored body of the macro. This pointer is returned.

Exceptional conditions: None.

Technical notes: The only note of interest is that this module realizes a search of the fixed-block-size directory. Usually a linear search will suffice, as most macro libraries are limited in size. However, other searches are possible that order the directory only and not the stored definitions. Sometime this module is merged with the argument list preparer.

Argument list preparer module

Input: The operand field of a macro call.

Output: The argument list to be used in expanding the macro.

General procedure: Using the form of the operand field (keyword or positional), the default values that appear in the definition, and the nondefault values that appear in the call, a list is produced containing the strings to be substituted for each parameter in the macro definition.

Exceptional conditions: Illegal syntax in the argument specifications, using a name in keyword specification that is not that of a parameter, and using illegal characters for arguments are typical of the types of errors that can occur here.

Technical notes: (1) Many macroprocessors restrict parameters and arguments to having only certain characters and so on (perhaps a subset of the allowable characters in the remaining macroassembly source). Both this module and the definition entry module must pay particular attention to this. Similarly, certain macroprocessors may prohibit, on general commonsense grounds, such arguments as *macro* and *end*. These error conditions must also be detected. (2) Basically the output of the module is a sequence of pairs of the form (parameter name, argument string).

Text generation module

Inputs: The body of a macro and a prepared argument list.

Output: The "expanded" body, obtained by substituting for each parameter in the body the corresponding argument string.

General procedure: Each line of the body is searched for the specially marked parameters, as prepared by the definition entry module. The parameters in the line, along with their special markers, are removed and are replaced by the entries appearing in the argument list.

Exceptional conditions: The primary type of error that can occur here is one of a "text editing" flavor—for example, the expanded line is too long.

Technical notes: The problems of text substitution are well known. Certain parameters become shorter and others longer when substitutions are done. There are, in certain macroprocessors, special characters called concatenation characters, which serve to "fuse together" pieces of text, and then disappear (see the Exercises). We leave to the Exercises some of the thinking that goes into text manipulation systems.

We do not discuss the error handler of I/O modules in the above form. There is little difference between their roles in macroprocessor design and assembler design. We do make the following comments however: Recall that the macroprocessor is a preprocessor to the assembler. Its input is a macroassembly program with macro definitions and calls. Its output is a "pure" assembly language program, devoid of both definitions and calls, the calls having been replaced with expanded text. It is the role of the input/output module, in part, to create these various I/O files and to properly interface with the user and assembler.

Executive module

In single-pass macroprocessing the basic sequence of module calls controlled by the executive module is the following: (1) Check each statement to see if it is a *.macro* statement. (2) If it is a *.macro* statement, pass it and all statements up to the matching *.endm* to the definition entry module. (3) If it is not a *.macro* statement, invoke the call recognition module to see if it is a call. (4) If it is a call, invoke the argument list preparer and then the text generation module to expand the call.

The executive module produces, in conjunction with the I/O module, an output file formed as follows: All noncalls or nondefinitions are passed to this output file in the order they occur in the source program. All expansions of calls are also passed to it, replacing the call statements. No definitions are passed at all.

What about the listing generator?

We have not explicitly discussed the listing generator in this development, primarily because of the preprocessor nature of the macro processor. In other words, we view the listing process as one controlled by the assembler's listing module. Usually, when macroprocessing ability is present, the assembler has directives for showing macro call expansions if the programmer desires to see them. In effect, the assembler has available to it for listing purposes both the input source to the macroprocessor and the output "pure" assembler source that it produces. The Exercises explore this further.

The data base

The primary data base for the macroprocessor is its directory-based table of macro definitions. The reader is led, through the Exercises, to mathematically model the directory-based table concept to attempt to justify it in macroprocessor design. Most of the remaining data structures used in the above modules are small and limited in scope—for example, a work area in which to prepare argument lists is required. The principal other data area necessary, in the case of recursive capabilities as outlined in the following section, is that of a stack—be it a hardware one or a software-simulated one.

11.5 Recursive Macro Capabilities

Let us recall the motivation for macro usage. A macro allows us to replace "structurally similar" sequences of code by a single parameterized invocation of an "instructionlike" entity. Thus, macros provide a kind of "extendability" to the assembly language, permitting us to define new sequences of operations and to view them as single "instructions." One of the significant features that most macroprocessors possess is that of recursive calling.

When recursive calling is present it works in the following context: Recall our notation of "line states" L0 and L1, as described in Section 11.3. As the macro is expanded and the state of line L is changed from L0 to L1, the macroprocessor, using the assembler-inherited format rules, attempts to view L1 as a formatted line of source and asks, "Is L1 a macro call, too?" If so, then it suspends its expansion of the (outer) macro and begins to expand the call contained in L1. This process continues, recursively, until the original, outermost macro has been fully expanded.

The tremendous advantage of recursive calling is that macros can be built out of smaller macros as well as out of ordinary assembly language statements. This ability is purely an "expressive one." Recursion is never needed, as all macros can be written nonrecursively.

Some thought on the part of the reader will reveal the following new implementation issues: (1) A much closer interplay between the format of the assembler source and the macro expansion process must be present in order to recognize nested calls. The expanded lines "l1" are not "just" lines of text any more, to be dealt with by the assembler. (2) When the macroprocessor "drops" what it is doing to recursively expand "inner" macros, it must use a stacklike structure to save information concerning the "dropped" macro; for example, it must save the prepared argument list and the position in the body where it was, and so on. Thus, recursive programming techniques must be brought to bear. (3) New limits must be placed on the user regarding allowable depths of recursion to avoid stack overflow.

A new module to handle recursive calling will thus have to be introduced, to be invoked by the text generation module, for handling recursive call expansion.

Some macroprocessors allow an even more subtle kind of recursion—recursive definition capability. The way this works is as follows: The body of the macro can contain properly nested pairs of *.macro* and *.endm* statements. Each of these "defines" an inner macro, whose name is usually a parameter of one of the outer macros. When the macro at level k is called for the first time, the nested definitions at level $k + 1$ are made. Thus one macro can "give birth" to families of similar macros, merely by virtue of its being called with different parameter values. This capability is truly a powerful one in that a cleverly selected core of macro definitions can lead to the automatic creation of a large macro library. We do not discuss this here, however, viewing it as beyond the scope of this text. It is sufficient to say, however, that with such an "expressive power," new rules concerning the presence of *.macro* and *.endm* strings within macro bodies must be invoked.

11.6 Concluding Remarks

This chapter has attempted to give an overview of the modular design issues related to macroprocessor realization. As in the preceding chapter, we have not attempted to explicitly "write" a macro processor, but rather to "set the stage" for writing one. In the Exercises for this chapter many of the concepts discussed above are explored in greater detail. After doing the Exercises, the reader should be able to begin thinking about implementing his or her own macroprocessor.

What are the steps needed to actually write one? We refer the reader to the discussion at the end of the previous chapter, for virtually the same comments apply here. In Appendix D we briefly describe those features of macroprocessors that have been omitted in our discussions here. In Appendix E we propose a simplified macroprocessor feature that extends the "SUBMAC" language introduced in Appendix C. This can be used as a model for student project design.

Exercises

Section 11.1

1. Review the macro facilities of the VAX/MACRO language by referring to the *VAX-11 MACRO Language Reference Manual* [18]. Try to specify which features are related to macro definitions, which to macro calls, and which to nested (recursive) features.

Section 11.2

2. How are macros defined in VAX/MACRO? How many parameters are allowed? What restrictions are there on the form of "symbol" and of "default value"?

3. Concerning bodies of macros in VAX/MACRO: What characters serve as delimiters in macro bodies? What other restrictions are there related to the content of macro bodies?

4. How are macros called in VAX/MACRO? Are both keyword and positional calls available? What kinds of restrictions are there on the form of call arguments?

5. (Difficult question.) The VAX/MACRO macroprocessor is closely "fused" to the VAX/MACRO assembler. (In fact, most people regard the fusion as "complete," in the sense that so many storage areas, modules, and so on are shared that it is really very hard to logically separate the two programs.) Say what you can about the format issue. How does the macroprocessor interpret statement format? Where are format errors caught during expansion—by the macroprocessor or by the assembler? You may have to write some small programs to test this out.

Section 11.3

6. (Fixed-block-size versus variable-block-size tables—see also exercise 13, part b, of Chapter 10.) Assume that the macro definitions table has to store up to n macro definitions, and that the sizes of macro definitions can range from $m1$ to $m2$ bytes. Try to develop, using mathematical reasoning, an answer to the following question: When is it more efficient from a time–storage product point of view to use a fixed-block-size table with $m2$ bytes per block as opposed to a variable-block-size table with some kind of directory or pointer structure for linking the blocks together? Do you think that variable-block-size tables are justified in macroprocessor design?

7. (Error handling) Using the *VAX/MACRO Reference Manuals* [18, 19], try to classify the various errors that are detected in the VAX/MACRO macroprocessor in the following categories: syntactic, errors during argument substitution, others. What others are possible?

8. (Single-pass design.) Can all assembly language programs be written without forward references, thus allowing single-pass assemblers to be practical? Answer this question in the context of the VAX/MACRO language first, with its myriad addressing modes. Then address the question in general.

9. Give an overall flowchart (informal) for the macroprocessor proposed in Section 11.3. Show the calls to each module identified in this section.

10. (Text generation.) One of the key issues in macroprocessor design is the text substitution issue—in particular, the problem of substituting for one string in a line another string of a possibly different length. Give an algorithm for replacing a specially delimited parameter in a line L by another string. Assume that the resulting line must not be longer than some maximum length and detect violations of this as an error.

Section 11.4

11. (Definition entry module.) Should the *.macro* and *.endm* parts of the macro definition be stored in the macro definitions table? What would be the advantages, if any, of doing this?

12. (Definition entry module.) Suppose that we want to allow macros to be redefined at will by the user, subject to the condition that it is always the most current definition (latest in the source code) that applies. How should this feature be implemented? What are the advantages of the directory-based approach here?

13. (Definition entry module.) We have talked about specially marking the parameters during macro definition entry to facilitate expansion. How should this marking be done? In particular, why isn't the already present set of delimiters sufficient here? This

is a general question which seeks to develop a feel for "efficiency" issues in software. Does this "special marking" impose any restrictions on the user of the macro facility?

14. (Definition entry module.) Propose a specific directory-based table organization for a macroprocessor and write a VAX/MACRO program (or a high-level language program) to implement searching and entry procedures.

15. (Definition entry module.) What kinds of exceptional conditions should be detected in the definition entry module. Why should they be viewed as exceptional?

16. (Call recognition module.) Some macroprocessors allow the user to define macros having the same names as machine operations. What is the impact of such "flexibility," if any, on a call recognition module? Why would one want to have such a capability? Discuss this issue in terms of the "integrated" macroassemblers described in this chapter.

17. (Call recognition module—see also exercise 12.) If we allow multiply defined macros, how does this impact on the call recognition module? How does this module know which definition is the most recent one?

18. (Argument list preparer module.) The argument list preparer is indeed a very independent module, working from two lists—a default list and an argument list. Write a preparer in the language of your choice, trying to incorporate the restrictions on arguments, default values, and symbol names, in VAX/MACRO. What kind of exceptional conditions should be detected?

19. (Argument list preparer.) Keyword and positional notations are usually not allowed to be mixed. Why? Develop a theoretical model of the two notations, involving assumptions about the number of parameters, size of arguments, and so forth, to answer the following general question: If a macro with m parameters is called k times in a program, and on the average, L parameters are specified, when is keyword format preferable to positional format? Use processing time and storage space requirements in formulating your answer.

20. (Text generation module—see also exercise 10.) Why are concatenation characters useful in macroprocessing? How does their presence affect text editing? In particular, when a concatenation character is "suppressed," should the text to its right be moved to the left, or should the text to the left be moved to its right? Does it matter?

21. (Text generation module.) We have spoken of the intimate link between the macroprocessor and the assembler format rules. We have noted that, in recursive macroprocessing settings (also review Section 11.5), during expansion of lines of the macro body, formatting is attempted. Discuss some of these issues in the context of text editing. In particular, can we write a text editor that directly outputs, as its expanded body line, four fields?

22. (Executive module and so on—see also exercise 9.) Give a more detailed flowchart of the single-pass macroprocessor showing error handling, listing generation, and module calls. Discuss some of the interfaces between the executive module and the called modules.

Section 11.5

23. Discuss the modifications that must be made to the macroprocessor to give it recursive calling capability in greater detail. In particular, define the "recursive call handler module" in the format used in Section 11.4 for the other modules.

24. If recursive calling is present and a hardware stack does not exist, one must be simulated in software. Write a program that simulates a software stack and the stack operations of push/pop.

25. What exactly must be saved in the stack used to implement recursive calls? Propose a format/organization for this saved material. In particular, since argument lists have to be saved, perhaps a variable-block-size entry in the stack should be made. How would this be implemented? (See also exercise 6.)

26. We have not discussed recursive definition capability at all, other than in a passing note. Why would this prove to be a useful capability to have? Would a recursive stacklike structure be needed to process nested definitions?

Chapter 12

Independent Assembly and Linking Issues

In this final chapter in Part II we will address the questions of independent assembly and linking in assembly language programming.

12.1 Introduction

What do we mean by "independent assembly" of subprograms? We mean, loosely speaking, the ability to write subprograms that "refer" to symbols external to them. Note that the assembler described in Chapter 10 did not possess this capability—external symbols were treated as undefined symbols and, as will be seen below, the requisite structures for effecting such external references were not present.

Thus we turn to the "global" features of assembly language. A "linker" will be needed to resolve (define) all external references and it is, in part, the design of such a linker that is of interest to us in this chapter.

Why do we want to have the ability to write programs and to assemble them, even though they refer to symbols in programs that may not, as yet, actually exist? The answer lies in the modular design philosophy that we have been espousing throughout this part of the text.

With such capability we can decompose a software design problem into distinct module design problems, each module symbolically referencing other modules for data, pointers, and other items. We can independently assemble the modules, thus minimizing syntactic debugging tasks. We can, within each module, use locally defined symbol names without concern as to their use in other modules (thus increasing expressive power). We can minimize "easily accessible" secondary storage requirements, since only object modules of previously assembled modules need be saved. Finally, we can make use of system/user-supplied library modules.

12.2   Mechanisms: Independent Assembly/Linking Capacity

The concepts of global symbols and entry points

Some mechanism must be available for permitting external references to be defined. In VAX/MACRO this is accomplished through the use of special assembler directives, such as *.global* or *.weak*. We refer the reader to the Exercises for the details of the VAX/MACRO global symbol facilities. In general, most assembly languages possessing independent assembly/linking features have two generic types of directives called *.global* and *.entry,* with general format as follows:

```
.global p1,...,pn
.entry p1,...,pn
```

Each of the *pj* is a symbol name; in the case of *.global* they are the names of symbols defined in other segments of code; in the case of *.entry* they are the names of symbols defined within the program segment that may potentially be referenced by other segments.

As will be seen in the ensuing sections of this chapter, the addition of these directives to a (macro) assembler and the resulting modifications to the object file allow a systems program called a "linker" to be written. This linker program serves to tie together or "link" independently assembled modules, resolve intermodule references, and create a single "fused" module which is often called a "load module." All of this will soon be explored. But first we address briefly the modifications needed to the (macro) assembler to accommodate and properly process these new directives.

Changes needed to accommodate the .global *and* .entry *directives*

Let us assume that at most one of each directive appears per module. (The Exercises explore generalizations of this.) We summarize below the changes needed in the (macro) assembler, leaving the details of individual module modifications to the reader.

Pass 1 of the assembler. A new symbol table, called the external symbol table, will be created. It will be filled with the names of all symbols appearing in either the *.global* or *.entry* directives. The symbols will be typed "G" or "E," depending on the directive, and, for type "E" symbols, their values, as defined in the segment of code (and appearing in the regular symbol table), will be entered.

Syntactical checks will be imposed to assure that the number of symbols of each type is less than some limit N and that certain reserved names are not used. Multiply-defined symbols must be avoided, and type "G" symbols cannot appear in the regular symbol table or as type "E" symbols.

Pass 2 of the assembler. After a search of the regular symbol table fails to show a successful "find," the error detection mechanism of the assembler is temporarily circumvented. The external symbol table is searched next. If a match is found here and is of type "G," then the global symbol is set to the value of 0 (or to some other convenient constant), but no error is flagged.

The external symbol table is coded into the object file as an integral part of it. In addition, the "segment length" is entered into the object file. Although several definitions of "segment length" are possible, we settle on a simple one for the purposes of this discussion: segment length = maximum location counter value encountered during the assembly process.

Although the above changes may seem rather involved at first reading, they are not all that complex to incorporate. This is left as an exercise to the reader. The fastidious reader may, furthermore, want to give some thought to the new types of error conditions that may arise and about how the listing module should be modified to include the external symbol table.

12.3   Linker Design Issues in General

With the above changes incorporated in the (macro) assembler we can proceed to define the functions of the linker more precisely:

1. *Input to linker:* a collection $m_1, \ldots, m_k$ of independently assembled modules or segments (in object form).
2. *The rule of fundamental significance:* if, in any segment a symbol appears in a *.global* directive, then it appears in another segment in an *.entry* directive.
3. *Output of linker:* a single-fused "load module" N with all external symbols defined and all modules, but possibly one, adjusted to a new relative starting address. (Recall that all modules are assembled as if they begin at virtual address 0—obviously some "relocation" must be done.) If one writes position-independent code, this need to adjust can be greatly minimized, if not completely eliminated.

Note: The inputs to the linker are in object form. These "object forms," as created by the modified assembler described above, consist of

The "conventional" object code of the assembler, that is, pairs of the form (relative address, contents at that address).
The external symbol table.
The relocation and linkage directory (see Section 12.4).
The segment length.

In particular, then, the linker has no access to any "locally" defined symbols of the program segment nor to any of the original source statements. It is thus a "postprocessor" to the assembler and its relationship, in system software terms, to macroprocessors and assemblers is as pictured in Figure 12-1. The linker thus can

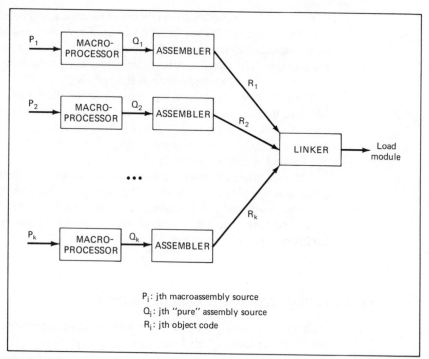

P_j : jth macroassembly source
Q_j : jth "pure" assembly source
R_j : jth object code

Figure 12–1.

be viewed as performing two distinct functions: (1) storage "allocation" and relocation, and (2) linkage. Let us describe these in greater detail.

Storage allocation and relocation of program segments

In a virtual memory machine like the VAX-11 the user does not need to know the physical memory addresses that a program runs in—nor does the assembler, for that matter. Nonetheless, with each module assembled as if its starting address were location 0, it is clear that possibly all but one of these modules will have to have their starting addresses shifted. What this, in turn, implies is that all absolute address references and all other address-dependent constants must be changed to reflect the new "starting" address. Intimately related to this concept is that of storage allocation. We have seen above that each segment m_j has an associated segment length l_j.

Clearly, to avoid conflict of memory locations and to be consistent with our choice for the definition of length, segment m_j must not begin before virtual address:

$$l_1 + \cdots + l_{j-1}$$

We are assuming that the order of linking is $m_1, \ldots, m_j$. We may make this assumption without any loss of generality. The above statement is true for j greater than 1; so the assigned starting addresses $a_1, \ldots, a_j$ must obey

$$a_1 \ >= \ 0$$
$$a_j \ >= \ l_1 + \cdots + l_{j-1} \quad \text{for} \quad j > 1$$

What relocation entails for segment m_j, then, is a shift in all address dependent values by a_j. Several related comments are in order at this time:

1. If we truly insist on position-independent code, as discussed above, all of the relocation need can disappear.
2. The specific values for the a_j may depend upon other criteria. For example, one may want each module to begin on a longword boundary or may want, say, 20 percent excess space in the module for "debugging" purposes. Thus although a_j can be as small as $l_1 + \cdots + l_{j-1}$, in general a larger value can appear.
3. Even if no relocation is necessary, the storage "allocation" has to be done.

Linkage

The function of linking is rather easy to describe. Recall two things from our earlier discussion. First, all symbols that are referenced in a module and that are declared in a *.global* directive are assembled as if their values were 0 or some other fixed constant.

Secondly, all such symbols must appear in *.entry* directives in other segments. Thus we can envision a two-pass process analogous to the process of program assembly.

Pass 1. Using the values of the a_j and using the external symbol table for each module, calculate the "true value" of each type "E" symbol (entry point). This value is a_j plus the value recorded in the external symbol table for module j.

Pass 2. Using these calculated "true values" for the entry points, all global references can now be resolved. Recall our restriction above about global symbols and entry points (our fundamental "rule"). This true value replaces 0 (or whatever convenient constant was chosen) and the machine code is suitably adjusted.

This table of "true values" of all entry points is often called the global symbol directory.

12.4   The Relocation and Linkage Directory

As a general rule linkers are much smaller programs than either assemblers or macroprocessors. Thus, the numbers of parts (or modules) needed to implement a linker are correspondingly fewer. Nonetheless, before we can propose a modular structure, we must address the somewhat ambiguous problem of relocation and position-independent code, as well as the requisite changes to the assembler, in more detail. Let us recall the definition of position-independent code. It is code written so that, regardless of where placed in virtual memory, it will function in exactly the same manner. If all symbolic addressing is done with relative addressing modes, then VAX users can generate such a code quite easily. Very often, however, a given assembler facility forces a user to use absolute addresses—such addresses are created under an assumed starting address, and these addresses have to change when the program is relocated. How do we implement such a change?

The modified assembler (see our remarks above) must make available in the object file a list of all locations where, because of the presence of address-dependent values, relocation has to be done. It usually does this by creating a table called a "relocation directory" whose elements are of the form:

```
address, relocation amount
```

address is the relative address at which a machine instruction or data-generating assembler directive was assembled. The *relocation amount* is the amount by which the assembled code has to be relocated. The Exercises will explore this latter concept more carefully, but let us give an example. Suppose that a program in some hypothetical assembly language has been assembled under assumed starting address 0, and that an absolute instruction like "load" 33 (load from address 33) has been assembled at location 57. Clearly, if this program is to be relocated to a new address a, the address field of the load instruction must be adjusted to read $a+33$. The "relocation amount" in this case is a, the "new" starting address. Were the program originally assembled at a starting address of 200 and contained at 262 a "load" 342 instruction, then the relocation amount for starting address a is $a–200$.

The "pairs" in the relocation directory in these cases would be respectively

```
57,*   and   262,*-200
```

where we have used the symbol "*" to denote the "real beginning" of the current program segment.

How does the assembler create this relocation directory? We leave many of the details of the ensuing brief discussion to the reader but make the following remarks:

1. The assembler has built into its semantic rules the concept of an absolute expression and a relative expression. Absolute expressions include, among other things, constant address references. Relative expressions include symbolic references assembled as offsets from the program counter.
2. During Pass 2 assembly, as object code is being created, the assembler thus generates a relocation directory entry for each "absolute" address reference.

A glance at the assembly language reference manual (e.g., ref. 18) for most sophisticated assemblers that permit "direct" address references indicates a complete variety of rules for deciding if an assembled instruction is to be "relocated" or not.

Let us thus highlight the real advantage of the relative addressing schemes (modes) of VAX/MACRO and the concept of position-independent code: no relocation directory need be created. Note that *.address* directives generate (obviously) address-dependent constants. These have to be adjusted during relocation: that is, code containing these directives may not be position-independent. The Exercises explore this further.

More on relocation: Integrating the relocation directory with linking

It is interesting to note that the relocation directory concept can be easily expanded to simplify the linking resolution problem as well. Let us make in what follows the reasonable assumption that all program segments are assembled at assumed relative address 0. (Certainly this is a reasonable assumption in a virtual memory system—even in a conventional system where relocation takes place it is reasonable.) Let us also assume, harking back to our remarks of Section 12.3, that all global symbol references are assembled as if they were references to address 0 (absolute).

Note that as a consequence of our first assumption all entries in the relocation directory are of the form:

```
address,*
```

and that, in effect, the "real beginning" of the segment has to be "added" to the assembled address to relocate the instruction. Note that we place the word "added" in quotes. In a "direct address" machine a real addition to the originally assembled address would take place. In machines with more complex addressing modes, it may be an offset or displacement which is "added" to. Suppose we assume, also, that every segment begins with a statement like:

```
segnm=.
```

and that *segnm* by default is an entry point of the segment—a special one called the "segment name." (*segnm* could be placed also in an *.entry* directive, or this may not be necessary.) This "artifice" ensures that the symbol *segnm* appears in the external symbol table, with value 0 and of type "E."

Now, under all of the above assumptions the relocation directory entries are in effect of the form *address,segnm,* with the "real beginning" of the segment being viewed as the "real value" of *segnm*. In other words, we add the value of *segnm* to correct the relocated instruction.

Once we realize this, it is easy to approach the linking problem as well. During Pass 2, when the assembler encounters a type "G" external reference, it also creates an entry, this time into a "linkage directory." The form of this entry is now

```
address,global_symbol_name
```

The meaning of this is that the assembled value of 0 for the global symbol is to be modified (by the linker) by adding the "true value" of the global symbol (as determined by Pass 1 of the linker).

The conclusion is that the relocation problem and the linking problem are in effect the same: Created addresses have to be modified by the addition of certain global symbol values—values to be created at link time. These global symbols are "genuine" (for linking purposes) or "artificial" (for relocation purposes).

In many systems, then, a single directory is in fact created by the assembler and is called something like "the relocation and linkage directory."

12.5 Modular Design Issues for Linkers

We finally are in a position to address the design of the linker itself. Because of its small size we have a limited number of modules, as seen below:

Global symbol directory creator (Pass 1)
Relocation/linking module (Pass 2)
Load module creator (Pass 2)
I/O module (Passes 1 and 2)

There is also an executive module which controls the linker "flow" and, possibly, an error handler module.

We undertake the specification of these modules in the same manner used in the previous two chapters. First we give a brief, functional description of each module (except for the executive module, which is described separately, and the error handler).

Global symbol directory creator. This module, invoked in Pass 1, calculates the "true values" for all type "E" global symbols and creates a master directory of these entry points and their values, called the "global symbol table." It does this by using the external symbol table of each module and the "segment lengths" of the modules.

Relocation/linking module. This module, invoked in Pass 2, modifies all relocatable address or external address references found in the object file of the segment by consulting the relocation and linkage directory of the segment.

Load module creator. This module, also invoked in Pass 2, moves the relocated/linked code of the object file (and all the remaining code as well) into the load module. That is, using the terminology of Section 12.3, the machine code at relative address r of segment m_j is moved (after possible relocation/linking) to relative location $a_j + r$ in the load module.

I/O module. Our discussion of this module is, again, very limited. It is invoked in Pass 1 to read in the object files to be linked together and in Pass 2 to write the load module into the appropriate file, and possibly the global symbol directory as well.

We follow these brief descriptions above with a more detailed look at the first three modules:

Global symbol directory creator

Inputs: The external symbol table of a module m_j, its segment length l_j, and a starting address a_j (relative address in the load module).

Outputs: An entry into the global symbol table for each type "E" symbol in the external symbol table. The form of the entry is (symbol name, $r + a_j$), where r is the relative address of the symbol appearing in the external symbol table of m_j. An updated "starting address" $a_{j+1} = f(a_j, l_j)$ is produced, too, for some function f (possibly as simple as $a_j + l_j$).

General procedure: The procedure is straightforward. The external symbol table for module m_j is searched. For each type "E" symbol found, a_j is added to the relative address r. This value, along with the symbol name, is entered into the global symbol table. A simple table entry/search procedure is assumed to be available. After all type "E" symbols in the external symbol table have been processed, a_{j+1} is calculated.

Exceptional conditions: Multiply defined type "E" symbols (i.e., type "E" symbols defined in two different segments) would be detectable by this module during its global symbol table entry phase. Also, if $r+a_j$ is, for some reason, too large for the system allocated load module addresses, an error would be flagged.

Technical notes: (1) We have not as yet discussed the format of the external symbol table produced by the assembler. Since this table is produced primarily for linker use, and only secondarily for user-visible listing purposes, this format should be set up for ease of use by the linker. For example, it could have two halves—one for type "E" symbols and one for type "G" symbols. A fixed block entry size in each half could simplify the search process. (2) The implementation of the rule $a_{j+1} = f(a_j, l_j)$ and the choice of f have been left vague. The Exercises will explore certain aspects of this problem.

Relocation/linking module

Inputs: The relocation and linkage directory of module m_j, the "conventional" object code" of m_j, and the global symbol table.

Outputs: An object file with all relocatable address and external address references correctly linked/relocated.

General procedure: Each entry in the relocation and linkage directory is examined in turn. Recall that it is of the form *address, symbol name*. The *symbol name* is searched for in the global symbol table. Its value is added to the appropriate field of the machine code in m_j assembled at relative address *address*, so as to relocate/link the machine code. This new machine code (so modified) replaces the "old" machine code at *address*.

Exceptional conditions: Recall rule 2 of Section 12.3: If a symbol appears in a *.global* directive of a segment, it must appear in a *.entry* directive in some other segment. If this rule has not been obeyed, the violation will be detected here—we will not always find an entry in the global symbol table for the symbol *symbol name*. Other exceptional conditions here are similar to the one cited above for the global symbol directory creator—for example, an address that is too large for the system-allocated load module space or too large to fit into the allocated machine code format (as chosen by the assembler).

Technical note: Again the format of the relocation and linkage directory can be chosen so as to maximize linker efficiency, as it is not primarily a user-visible file. The Exercises explore several possible format variations.

Load module creator

Inputs: An object module m_j suitably relocated/linked by the relocation/linking module; a "starting address" a_j.

Outputs: None.

General procedure: This is basically a block move routine which moves the modified machine code of module m_j to "location" a_j in memory. This value, a_j, is most likely an offset (relative address) from a base address that is to be determined at the time that the "load module" is loaded by the system.

Exceptional conditions: These, too, presumably relate to any attempts to move to addresses that are out of range. Acceptable load module addresses would most likely range from 0 to some limit *ldlm*. In fact, such errors would most likely be detected by the other modules, as already indicated. The designer has to resolve a "division of labor" issue here.

Technical notes: The produced "load module" looks like "pure object code," that is, the kind of code produced by the assembler of the type described in Chapter 10. With no relocation and linkage directory or external symbol table of its own it cannot be linked with other load modules and any further relocation must be "virtual" (i.e., done in hardware).

Some comments on the executive module

We can best summarize the action of the executive module as follows. The reader is asked, in the Exercises, to prepare a flowchart to reflect the ensuing discussion.

Pass 1. Select a_1 (see below). For $j=1, \ldots, k$ (k = number of segments) do the following: Call the global symbol table creator for module m_j with starting address a_j.

Pass 2. For $j=1, \ldots, k$ do the following: Call the relocation/linking module. Afterward call the load module creator.

Store the complete load module; optionally print out the global symbol table.

Note that a_1 must be selected by the executive module to initiate the global symbol directory creator call "loop." In a virtual memory system like that of the VAX, choosing a_1 to be 0 is a reasonable choice to make. We have not discussed at all the processing of detected errors. Presumably the same philosophy of our assembler chapter would hold. The executive module, upon detecting errors (via status return codes, for example), would call a central error handler module. Details are left to the reader.

12.6 Concluding Remarks

It is extremely important to remember that the linker design proposed here requires object files as inputs and not source files. The object files must contain external symbol tables, relocation and linkage directories, and information about "segment length." Nothing, however, requires that they necessarily be the object files of assembly language programs! It is common practice in modern operating system design to have various compilers, like FORTRAN or Pascal, produce object codes compatible with that of the system assembly language. Furthermore, high-level language source programs can call or refer to symbols in assembly language programs, and conversely. The point is that, from the point of view of the linker this is all irrelevant. It operates on object files. From the point of view of the individual compilers or assembler the linker itself is irrelevant—the compiler/ assembler designer need only know the "standard" object code format. Herein lies the great power of the independent assembly philosophy, which might be termed better as the "independent object code" philosophy.

Exercises

Section 12.1

1. Look at the *VAX/MACRO Language Reference Manual* [18]. Identify those features of the language that are "global" as opposed to "intrinsic" or "macro-related." Tie your discussion into default conventions, if necessary.

2. Again by consulting the VAX systems manuals describe how the *link* command works. What kinds of restrictions on its use are present?

Section 12.2

3. Refer also to exercise 1, above. Describe the *.global* and *.entry* directives in VAX/ MACRO. What kinds of rules are there concerning their use? You may ignore the *.weak* directive.

4. This exercise focuses on the changes needed in Pass 1 of the assembler.
   a. Does it matter how many *.global* or *.entry* directives are allowed per segment? Explain how to handle multiple directives.
   b. Propose a format for the external symbol table. Do you think that it should be ordered and searched logarithmically or that a linear search of an unordered table is sufficient?
   c. What kinds of names for external symbols should be considered "reserved" or illegal? Why?

5. This exercise focuses on the changes needed for Pass 2 of the assembler.
   a. Propose another "reasonable" definition for segment length. Why is the concept of "segment length" an important one?
   b. Can you think of any kind of possible "forward referencing" restriction on global symbols—for example, a type "G" symbol cannot be referred to unless it has appeared in a preceding *.global* directive? Is such a restriction needed? Would it be useful/convenient to have one? What implications on the assembler's design would it have?

6. Again the assembler: Propose two new modules called the "external symbol table creator" and the "global symbol search module." Define their functions in a fashion analogous to what was done in Chapter 10, being certain to consider possible exceptional conditions. We have deliberately left their names a bit vague to allow maximum flexibility. Be sure that all the important Pass 1 and Pass 2 extensions are covered by these modules.

Section 12.3

7. Define "position-independent code." How can you guarantee that a VAX/MACRO program is position-independent?

8. (Relocation.) Do we really ever want to have an excess of, say, 20 percent? Why would this be useful? How does it relate to alternative definitions of segment length, and should the problem of "excess space" be resolved at the assembly level or at the linker level?

9. (Linking.) Based upon the brief discussion at the end of Section 12.3, draw an informal flowchart of the linking process. Is a two-pass process really needed? To allow a one-pass linker, what restrictions on global references are required?

Section 12.4

10. Does VAX/MACRO have a concept of absolute and relocatable symbols/expressions? What are the definitions used?

11. The problem of deciding which symbols are absolute is not an easy one. Consider the assignment statement *x=5*. If the programmer later writes

    ```
    .byte x
    ```

    then this directive seems to be "absolute"; that is, the programmer really intends to have a byte with value 5 at this location. If he had written instead, however,

    ```
    x: .byte 0
    ```

    and then the *.byte x* directive, is it still an absolute reference? How should this kind of analysis be handled? (General discussion.)

12. Propose a format for the relocation and linkage directory. Are the actual "names" of the symbols required in the directory, or can some kind of "index position" in the external symbol table be used to minimize table size?

Section 12.5

13. (Global symbol directory creator.) Using the language of your choice and the format of your choice for the external symbol table, code a global symbol directory creator. What choice of the function f are you making?

14. (Symbol conflict.) Why do multiply-defined global symbols pose a problem? Can conflicts arise if one of them is of type "E," the other of type "G"? Are there conflicts between local symbols (not declared in *.entry* or *.global* directives) and global ones? Explain.

15. (Relocation/linking module.) It was stated in Section 12.5 that this module, based upon the value found in the global symbol table, relocates/links by adjusting (adding to) the address field in the machine code. How is this to be done, in particular, in VAX/MACRO? Relate your answer to addressing modes and to the concepts of relocatability in VAX/MACRO.

16. (Relocation/linking module.) Using the language of your choice and the format of your choice, code a simple relocator/linker. You need not write the "adjusting" part of this routine—leave it as a dummy call. How do you detect/treat the error of a type "G" symbol that was not defined as a type "E" symbol in some segment?

17. The load module creator is essentially a block move routine producing "pure object code." We have stated that no further software relocation can be done here. Discuss the reasons why if you agree with the statement just made.

18. How does the executive module know when one object segment ends and another begins or when all k of them have been read? Relate this need to a possible minor modification to the already modified assembler.

Appendix A

Terminals, Editors, and Programs

This section describes the steps needed to access the VAX from a terminal and to create, assemble, link, execute, and view the results of an assembly language program. The commands described are for the operating system VMS, version 2; these commands may differ slightly on other versions of VMS. If the reader is using a VAX with a different operating system from VMS, the commands will most certainly differ. In this case the reader may want to consult his or her computation center or instructor for help in implementing steps 0–6. For VMS, the steps are listed below and then described in detail:

Step 0: Login.
Step 1: Create a source program using one of the system editors.
Step 2: Assemble the program. Reassemble after correcting any errors.
Step 3: Load (actually *link*) the assembled program.
Step 4: Execute the linked program.
Step 5: Use the system debugger to examine the contents of the locations containing "answers."
Step 6: Logout.

Step 0: Login

Login is the term used to describe the procedure of accessing the computer from a terminal. In order to log in, we need two items: a user name and a password. These can be supplied by the instructor or by the people in charge of the computer system. Once you have a user name and a password and have found a terminal to use:

a. Press the return key—it may be marked "ret" or "new line."

b. The system will type "username:".

c. Type in your user name; then press the return key.

d. The system will type "password:".

e. Type in your password; then press the return key. *Note!!* . . . The password is not printed out by the system.

f. Some sort of message of greeting will appear and then a dollar sign ($). The $ indicates that you are "logged in" and the system is ready to accept commands. In fact, this is called *command mode*.

The following shows a typical login:

```
username:   lemone
password:
              Northeastern Univ. VAX/VMS V2.3
    $
```

The login procedure described here is for terminals which are already connected to the computer. If the terminal is not connected to the computer, it must be connected via a telephone line. Instructions for doing this may be found near the terminal. If there are no instructions, your instructor or the people in charge of your computer system can give directions.

We are now ready to type in an example assembly language program.

Step 1:   Create a source program using one of the system editors

A source program is a program before it has been assembled (or compiled). Our source program will be written in VAX assembly language. An editor helps to type in and correct source programs. Most systems have more than one editor from which to choose. Some common editors on the VAX are TECO, EDT, and SOS. We will describe SOS here and use it to create our assembly language program. You may wish to get documentation on some of the other editors available on your system. To begin typing in your assembly language program:

a. Type:

```
edit/sos something.mar
```

Here, *something* can be any name consisting of up to nine letters or digits. *Something* then becomes the name of a file—a file can be thought of as a container of information. This information is now stored under the name *something* and can be accessed under this name until the programmer issues a command to delete the file. The three letters after the "." represent the file type. Here, *mar* is the file type since *mar* is the file type for an assembly language program. (*for* is the file type for a FORTRAN program, *pas* is the file type for a Pascal program, etc.)

b. SOS will supply a line number—this is just for editing and does not appear in the program itself.

c. Type in your assembly language program. Press return after each line.

d. When the entire program has been typed in, press the escape key, <ESC>. (<ESC> prints as a "$".)

e. SOS now prints a "*" indicating that changes may be made to the program.

f. If there are no changes to be made, type *e*. A "$" should appear. You are now "out of" the SOS editor. You are now back "in" command mode (See Figure A–1).

The program in Figure A–1 is the program discussed in Chapter 1 that computes

```
result:=a*b+c
```

when $a = 2$, $b = 3$, and $c = 4$. Note that in line 1000 *sturt* was mistakenly typed rather than *start*.

It is possible to make corrections while a line is being typed in; just press the DELETE key (<DEL>). This backspaces and deletes the previous character. If the line has too many errors, it may be reentered by holding down the <CTRL> key and pressing the "u" key. This is denoted <CTRL>U and prints as ^U. There is a "^" key on the keyboard. Don't be misled into thinking it is the same as the <CTRL> key. They merely print out the same. (The same is true for "$" and <ESC>—they both print out as "$".) Note also that the <CTRL> must be held down *while* the "u" key is being pressed. It doesn't work if they are pressed one at a time! <CTRL>U wipes out the entire line, but it still may be typed in anew. After the return key has been pressed, it is too late to do this. The editing commands may be used to make changes, however.

To make changes to an assembly language program already typed in, type:

```
edit/sos something.mar
```

Figure A–1.

```
$ edit/sos  kalcl.mar
Input: DBA1:[LEMONE]KALC1.MAR;1
00100    a:         .long    2
00200    b:         .long    3
00300    c:         .long    4
00400    result:    .long
00500    start:     .word
00600               movl     a,r6
00700               mul12    b,r6
00800               add13    c,r6,result
00900    last:      ret
01000               .end     sturt
01100    $
*e
[DBA1:[LEMONE]KALC1.MAR;1]
$
```

The SOS editor types a "*" indicating it is ready for any of the following editing commands.

a. p(rint)
b. f(ind)
c. s(ubstitute)
d. r(eplace)
e. d(elete)
f. i(nsert)
g. n(renumber)
h. e(nd)

a. *p n* instructs SOS to print line *n*. It also means SOS is ready to make corrections to the line indicated.

EXAMPLE

    p 1000

This instructs the editor to print line 1000; the "substitute" command may now be used on line 1000 if changes are desired.

b. fstring<*ESC*> instructs SOS to find the first occurrence of *string in* or *after* the current line. (If *p 1000* has been typed, then the current line is 1000.) The escape key must terminate this command. (Remember the escape key <ESC> prints as "$".)

EXAMPLE

    fsturt$

This instructs SOS to find the string *sturt*. Changes may now be made to the line containing *sturt*.

c. sstring1<*ESC*>string2<*ESC*> instructs SOS to substitute *string2* for all occurrences of *string1* in the current line.

EXAMPLE

    ssturt$start$

SOS substitutes *start* for *sturt*.

d. *r n* instructs SOS to replace line *n*.

EXAMPLE

```
r 1000
```

SOS deletes line 1000 and prints 1000; a new line 1000 may now be typed in.

e. *d n* instructs SOS to delete line *n*.

EXAMPLE

```
d 1000
```

SOS deletes line 1000.

f. *i n* instructs SOS to insert a new line at or after line *n*.

EXAMPLE

```
i 900
```

SOS prints a number (equal to or greater than 900—if there is a line 900, the new line will be inserted after line 900) and waits for that line to be typed in. Sometimes after many insertions there are no more numbers to be used less than the next number. The following command rectifies this.

g. *n* instructs SOS to renumber all the lines in the program.

h. *e* instructs SOS to terminate. A $ should appear. It is usually best to terminate with *eb*. The *b* tells SOS not to save the old version of the program.

This section is a (brief!) introduction to entering and correcting source programs (editing). For further information, see the following manuals (your computer center should have copies): *VAX/VMS Primer* [20] and *VAX-11 Text Editing Reference Manual* [27].

In addition, there may be documentation on one of the other system editors (e.g., EDT or TECO).

We are now ready to assemble our program.

Step 2: Assemble the program

To assemble a VAX-11 MACRO program, type:

```
macro/enable=debug/lis something
```

where *something* is the name of the program created in step 1. */enable=debug* indicates that we will be using the debugger to look at "answers" when we execute the program. */lis* puts a listing of the assembled version into a file called *something.lis*.

EXAMPLE

```
macro/enable=debug/lis kalc1
```

assembles the program *kalc1*. *kalc1.lis* now contains a listing of the machine code for *kalc1.mar*.

Programs can be printed out *on the terminal* by typing *type something*.

EXAMPLE

```
type kalc1.mar
```

types the source program out on the terminal.

EXAMPLE

```
type kalc1.lis
```

types out the assembled listing of *kalc1* on the terminal.

Programs can be printed out *on paper* (called "hardcopy" in computer jargon) by typing *print something*.

EXAMPLE

```
print kalc1.mar
```

causes the source program to be printed on the system printer.

Step 3: Link the assembled program

The linker determines the addresses where the program is to be stored. Linking can also be used to link more than one assembled or compiled program into one single program:

```
link/debug something
```

/debug means to link the debugger to our assembled program.

EXAMPLE

```
link/debug kalc1
```

links program *kalc1* and the debugger.

Step 4: Execute the linked program

To execute (run) the linked program, type

```
run something
```

where *something* is the name of the linked program.

EXAMPLE

```
run kalcl
```

Step 5: Use the system debugger

The symbolic debugger is itself a program that enables the programmer to debug his or her own programs interactively, that is, during execution. It can also be used to examine the contents of various locations during execution. It is perhaps the simplest way to check that the program is calculating correct answers. By setting breakpoints—addresses at which the program will stop execution, the programmer can examine the contents at various stages of execution. Chapters 7 and 8 discuss other, more standard ways of "printing out" answers. The contents of locations may be printed out in hexadecimal (the default mode), in decimal, in octal, or in ASCII (characters). The following are a small subset of the instructions available:

set mode dec(imal): The contents of locations are displayed as decimal numbers rather than as hexadecimal numbers.

set mode hex(adecimal): Values are displayed as hexadecimal numbers. Other useful modes are *ascii, address,* and *octal.*

set break label: Execution is stopped the first time *label:* is encountered.

EXAMPLE

```
set break last
```

stops execution at label *last:*.

go: This initiates execution.

ex(amine) symbolic-name: the contents of location symbolic-name are displayed.

EXAMPLE

```
ex result
```

prints the contents of location *result*.

set ty(pe) word: The debugger looks at a word of data rather than a longword. Other useful types that can be set are *long* (the default) and *byte*.

exit: This returns control to the operating system.

Figure A–2.

```
username:        lemone
password:
      Northeastern Univ. VAX/VMS  V2.1
$ edit/sos kalc1.mar
Input: DBA1:[LEMONE]KALC1.MAR;1
00100    a:         .long    2
00200    b:         .long    3
00300    c:         .long    4
00400    result:    .long
00500    start:     .word
00600               movl     a,r6
00700               mull2    b,r6
00800               addl3    c,r6,result
00900    last:      ret
01000               .end     sturt
01100    $
*e
[DBA1]:[LEMONE]KALC1.MAR;1]
$ macro/enable=debug/lis kalc1
                        0021  1000           .end      sturt
%MACRO-E-UNDEFXFRAD, Undefined transfer address           !
$ ed/sos kalc1.mar
Edit: DBA1:[LEMONE]KALC1.MAR;1
*ssturt$start$
01000               .end     start
*e
[DBA1:[LEMONE]KALC1.MAR;2]
$ macro/enable=debug/lis kalc1
$ link/debug kalc1
$ run kalc1
          VAX-11 DEBUG Version 2.00
%DEBUG-I-INITIAL, language is MACRO, module set to '.MAIN.'
DBG>set mode dec
DBG>set break last
DBG>go
start at .MAIN.\START+2
break at .MAIN.\LAST
DBG>ex result
.MAIN.\RESULT:   10
DBG>exit
$ logout
$
```

Step 6:   Logout

   logout is the command for disconnecting the terminal from the computer.

   EXAMPLE

       $ logout

Figure A–2 shows steps 1–6 for the program that calculates

   result:=a*b+c

Figure A–3.

```
username:       lemone
password:
             Northeastern Univ. VAX/VMS   V2.1
$ edit/sos tenfact.mar
Input: DBA1:[LEMONE]TENFACT.MAR:1
00100   ;
00200   ;
00300   ;  this program calculates 10 factorial (10!)
00400   ;
00500   fact:   .long
00600   ;
00700   begin:  .word
00800           movl    #1,fact      ;fact=1
00900           movl    #1,r6        ;i=1
01000   loop:   mull2   r6,fact      ;fact=fact*i
01100           aobleq  #10,r6,loop  ;i=i+1
01200   last:   ret
01300           .end    begin
01400   $
*e
[DBA1:[LEMONE]TENFACT.MAR;1]
$ macro/enable=debug/lis tenfact
$ link/debug tenfact
$ run tenfact
             VAX–11 DEBUG Version 2.00
%DEBUG–I–INITIAL, language is MACRO, module set to '.MAIN.'
DBG>set mode dec
DBG>set break last
DBG>go
start at .MAIN.\BEGIN+2
break at .MAIN.\LAST
DBG>ex fact
.MAIN.\FACT:   3628800
DBG>exit
$ logout
$
```

Note that when the operating system is waiting for an instruction, it types $. When the (SOS) editor is waiting for an instruction, it types *. When the debugger is waiting for an instruction, it types DBG>. Figure A–3 shows steps 1–6 for the program that calculates 10-factorial.

Formatting

DEC recommends the following basic format for readable programs:

Label	Operation	Operand(s)	; Comments
↑	↑	↑	↑
Column 1	Column 9	Column 17	Column 33

The columns correspond to the tab positions on most terminals. We recommend indenting some operations beyond column 9, particularly within loop structures, to improve readability.

Instructions may be continued onto the next line by using a hyphen.

EXAMPLE

```
movl    longoperand, —
        longeroperand
```

Appendix B

Design Issues Not Examined in Chapter 10

The purpose of this appendix is twofold. We wish to, first, identify, in list form, some of the items of "real" assembler design that we did not examine in Chapter 10. Secondly, we wish to give the reader, through the Exercises to this appendix, an opportunity to deal with the incorporation of these ideas into the mainstream of Chapter 10.

We have not discussed in Chapter 10 the following features of VAX/MACRO vis-à-vis their assembly:

1. Local symbols (labels).
2. Radix conversion issues ($^\wedge$D, $^\wedge$O, etc.).
3. Implementation of default sizes in addressing modes.
4. All of the issues of listing generation (table of contents, titles, etc.).
5. *psect's*.
6. Register mask creation.
7. Restrictions on program length, table sizes, and so on.
8. Full details on error processing and fatal/nonfatal issues for errors.
9. Conditional assembly.

Exercises

1. Review the definition of "local symbol" in VAX/MACRO. Propose a separate module for handling their evaluation. What are the issues? How is the "range of definition" of a local symbol to be implemented?
2. Radix conversion is best viewed as a utility that can be called upon by the expression evaluator and other modules. Register mask creation can be viewed as part of the utility

module's function also. Give a general functional description of this ability and discuss some of the issues involved in conversion.

3. Discuss the purpose/implementation of default conventions in addressing modes. (We did so but briefly in Chapter 10.)

4. By consulting the VAX-11 *MACRO Language Reference Manual* [18] identify all of the options/features of the listings that can be produced. Identify the assembler directives that control the listings and discuss the issues involved in listing generator design. (See exercise 23 of Chapter 10 also.)

5. What is a *psect*? How should the concept be implemented in our *intrinsic* assembler design?

6. Discuss some of the "nuts and bolts" of assembler design like limits on program length, number of allowed symbols, and so on. How does the incorporation of such constraints affect what we have discussed in Chapter 10?

7. Why are some errors fatal, some nonfatal? How must nonfatal errors be dealt with to allow assembly to finish? What kind of "default" assumptions have to be made?

Appendix C

A Subset of VAX/MACRO for Trial Assembler Design: SUBMAC

In this appendix we attempt to define a subset of the VAX/MACRO language suitable for student assembler design projects. The language we define will be called SUBMAC, and it is essentially a restricted form of VAX/MACRO containing enough features to allow the techniques of Chapter 10 to be meaningfully applied, but not containing the myriad little details that tend to obscure assembler design.

As a pedagogical note it might be worthwhile to point out that authors of assembly language books usually approach the problem of selecting a language to "implement" in one of two ways. Either they "invent" a language, similar to a variety of common assembly languages but nonetheless "hypothetical" on a "hypothetical" computer, or they select a "subset" of an existing language, perhaps adding to it some features they would like to have. We follow this latter approach.

Since the SUBMAC language is basically a subset of VAX/MACRO, we refer the reader to the *VAX/MACRO Language Reference Manual* [18] for complete definitions and details. We focus below on the differences (restrictions) of SUBMAC. We organize the discussion below along the lines of the VAX/MACRO language reference manuals.

Format

The SUBMAC format is exactly as in VAX/MACRO, but there are no continuation lines or blank lines. Thus all statements must fit into one line. The standard statement format of VAX/MACRO applies. We further assume that all lines are no more than 80 characters, not counting the carriage return/linefeed. We further restrict the label field to between 1 and 7 characters, and restrict the types of characters in the fashion described below in the "Symbols" section. The last character of the label field, as in VAX/MACRO, must be a colon, ":". The remaining characters must form a user-defined symbol of SUBMAC. No global symbols exist in SUBMAC.

Character set

The character set in SUBMAC is also a restricted form of that of VAX/MACRO. Upper and lowercase letters are not distinguished from one another, and the following other symbols are used:

```
0 1 2 3 4 5 6 7 8 9 . : = tab space
# @ , ; + − / ^ [ ] ( ) < >
```

Numbers

Only integers are allowed in SUBMAC, and only the data types of byte, word, and longword. All restrictions on these integers are as in VAX/MACRO.

Symbols

There are two disjoint classes of symbols in SUBMAC—permanent symbols and user-defined symbols. The permanent symbols are the instruction and assembler directive mnemonics and the following symbols: R0, R1, . . ., R15, AP, FP, SP, PC.

User-defined symbols are symbols of one to six characters in length, made up of alphanumeric characters (A–Z, 0–9) and beginning with a letter. All symbols in the operation field must be permanent symbols. All symbols in the operand field are either user-defined symbols or register names. No local symbols exist in SUBMAC.

Terms and expressions

These definitions are very similar to those in VAX/MACRO. A "term" is either a number, a symbol, $^\wedge$A, or $^\wedge$M, followed by appropriate text or a number preceded by a unary radix operator. Terms (and expressions, defined next) can only appear in the operand field of statements or in assignment statements. Terms and expressions are evaluated as longwords.

"Expressions" are very limited in SUBMAC. They are of the form: +term, −term, term + term, or term − term.

Forward references

An expression is said to contain a forward reference to a symbol if the definition of the symbol appears in the source program after the statement in which the expression occurs. There are certain restrictions on the use of forward references in expressions, restrictions that will be described below. They relate to the need to guarantee that all symbols can be defined in the first pass of the assembly process.

Unary radix operators

These are exactly as in VAX/MACRO but limited to: ^B, ^D, ^O, and ^X. The "^" must be immediately next to the B, D, O, or X. ^A and ^M are special operators, subject to the behavior they have in VAX/MACRO with the following additional restrictions: the delimiter in ^A may be any legal character but space, tab, or ";".

Assignment statements

Only one definition of a symbol per program may be made with an assignment statement, contrary to the multiple-definition rule of VAX/MACRO. No forward references are allowed in assignment statements. All other restrictions of VAX/MACRO apply. In particular, an assignment statement is viewed as being in the label field.

Current location counter

No use of the symbol "." as the current location counter value is allowed in SUBMAC. Thus all changes to the location counter are implicit or via assembler directives.

Addressing modes

All addressing modes of VAX/MACRO are present in SUBMAC, except for general mode addressing. The following special comments are made. For all other rules the reader should refer to the VAX/MACRO language reference manuals. (Obviously in SUBMAC the types of expressions etc. usable in addressing modes are somewhat restricted, but the availability of the mode is as in VAX/MACRO.)

On displacement mode: The default displacement in SUBMAC is one word; if the SUBMAC assembler cannot fit the expression value into one word, then it considers it an error. Also, if the displacement evaluates to 0 and no length is specified, then register deferred mode is used.

On relative and relative deferred mode: The default displacement used for expressions is determined by the *.default* directive. If no such directive is present, then it is taken to be a longword. Recall that the need for default values arises when expressions contain forward references and cannot thus be evaluated in Pass 1; to allow the assembly process to continue an assumed memory allocation must be made.

Assembler directives

The following assembler directives are allowed in SUBMAC:

```
.show     .nshow    .default
.byte     .word     .long     .address
.ascii    .ascic    .ascid    .asciz
.blka     .blkb     .blkl     .blkw
.end
```

All restrictions on VAX/MACRO apply with the further restrictions of expressions and so forth implied by SUBMAC constraints. The following additional comments hold: On *.show* and *.nshow* only the "no argument" form is allowed—with the list count nonnegative, the listing is made; when negative, no listing is made, except in the case of an error.

Allowable instructions

The following instructions are allowed in SUBMAC. All other restrictions of VAX/MACRO and SUBMAC apply to their use.

```
acbb, acbl, acbw, addb2, addb3, addl2, addl3, addw2, addw3,
   aobleq, aoblss, ashl
beql, beqlu, bgeq, bgequ, bgtr, bgtru, bleq, blequ, blss,
   blssu, bneq, bnequ, brb, brw, bsbb, bsbw, bvc, bvs
callg, calls, caseb, casel, casew, clrb, clrl, clrw, cmpb,
   cmpc3, cmpc5, cmpl, cmpw, cvtbl, cvtbw, cvtlb, cvtlw,
   cvtwb, cvtwl
decb, decl, decw, divb2, divb3, divl2, divl3, divw2, divw3
ediv, emul
incb, incl, incw
jmp, jsb
locc
matchc, mcomb, mcoml, mcomw, mnegb, mnegl, mnegw, movab,
   moval, movaw, movb, movc3, movc5, movl, movw, movzbl,
   movzbw,
   movzwl, mulb2, mulb3, mull2, mull3, mulw2, mulw3
popr, pushab, pushal, pushaw, pushl, pushr
ret, rotl, rsb
sbwl, skpc, sobgeq, sobgtr, subb2, subb3, subl2, subl3,
   subw2, subw3
tstb, tstl, tstw
xorb2, xorb3, xorl2, xorl3, xorw2, xorw3
```

Program organization

There are no *psect*'s in SUBMAC, other than the single one defined by the program itself. The program terminates with an *.end* directive. The programs of SUBMAC are only "main programs," and the *.end* directive must contain the transfer point for execution. Subprograms and procedures may be written in SUBMAC, but they cannot be independently assembled and are thus part of the same program. They may, however, be invoked by *callg* and so forth, and register masks should be used.

Further comments

It may seem to the reader that we have stripped away so much power of VAX/MACRO as to render the SUBMAC language useless for writing programs. Some reflection will show that, although we have defined a language with less expressive ability, we can still write programs to perform a variety of useful functions. Our goal here, in any case, has been to define a language suitable for assembler design purposes. Once the reader fully understands these issues in the context of SUBMAC, he or she may feel free to augment its capacities.

We have, nonetheless, omitted in our specification of SUBMAC the following items which have to be resolved in order to complete an assembler for it:

Errors—what kinds and what is to be done about them.

I/O issues.

Restrictions on program length, table sizes, and so on (and *myriad details,* which the reader will encounter in the design process).

Appendix D

More Design Features for Macroprocessors

We list below some features often found in macroprocessors that we have chosen to overlook in Chapter 11.

1. *Nested definitions* (but see Section 11.5 for a very brief discussion).
2. *Conditional assembly and macroprocessors* (also see our comments in Appendix B). Conditional assembly is, in fact, a concept independent of macroprocessing, but for most "beginners" the two are usually intimately linked together. It is indeed true that often the most powerful "expressive" power of macros arises when conditional statements appear within the body.
3. *Created local labels*. These allow the user to have labels inside macro bodies that are not parameters of the macro, but to avoid the problem of "multiply defined" labels when macros are called more than once. (See the Exercises below.)
4. *String operators*. These are present in VAX/MACRO, and when used in conjunction with conditional assembly give a very powerful macro expansion capability.
5. *Repeat blocks* and similar constructs useful in creating "one-argument" macros.
6. *Opdef*'s and similar assembler directives for defining "new" opcodes.

Exercises

1. Why are the created local labels of VAX/MACRO needed? Are they needed? If we wanted to introduce such a facility into a macroprocessor, which of the modules discussed in Chapter 11 would need to be changed and how?

2. Reread Chapter 9 and also read about "conditional assembly" in the *VAX/MACRO Language Reference Manual* [18] and address the following two questions:

Why is it useful in macroprocessing?

What effect, if any, does its presence have on the design of the macroprocessor?

Appendix E

Adding Macro Features to SUBMAC

In this appendix we complement Appendix C by adding a macro capability to SUBMAC, the simplified version of VAX/MACRO.

We point out here the restrictions of SUBMAC/MACRO vis-à-vis the VAX/MACRO language.

Limits on arguments; body length restrictions. Consistent with SUBMAC format restrictions and available memory, limits must be set on both the number of allowable macro parameters (formal arguments) and on the number of allowed statements per macro body. These SUBMAC restrictions will be set by the student writing the macroprocessor.

Macro names. Macro names must obey all rules and conventions of SUBMAC user-defined symbols and must be distinct from other user-defined symbols.

Macro bodies; parameters. Macro bodies are made up of characters from the SUBMAC character set plus the character "!", which is a concatenation character. Parameters must be user-defined symbols, separated by commas and delimited by nonalphanumeric characters in the SUBMAC character set or by "!" in the macro body.

Order of search. To recognize calls the SUBMAC macroprocessor first searches the macro definitions directory, rather than some preset table of machine mnemonics/assembler directives. Thus the user may have macros that have the same names as SUBMAC permanent symbols.

Libraries. There are no macro libraries in SUBMAC.

String operators/arguments. There are none in SUBMAC.

Repeat blocks. There are none in SUBMAC.

Recursion. Nested calls are allowed; nested definitions are not. The student must determine the limit on nesting depth based upon allowable stack size. For students who have not had much recursive programming experience, a version of SUBMAC without nested calls might be considered.

Listings. The *.show* and *.nshow* directives in the assembler have forms with argument *me* for allowing macro expansions to be shown/suppressed.

Call/default arguments; positional/keyword forms. Call/default arguments are user-defined symbols or are null. Both positional and keyword argument calls are available. They cannot be mixed in SUBMAC.

Argument concatenation. The same rules as in VAX/MACRO apply.

"Numeric values." No passed numeric values are allowed in SUBMAC.

Created local labels. As in VAX/MACRO, this is an optional feature of SUBMAC. If used, then "$" and "?" must be added to the character set of SUBMAC for compatibility with VAX/MACRO.

Macro directives. Subject to the above restrictions and to those of VAX/MACRO, the following two directives are available:

```
.macro
.endm
```

Macro redefinitions. Macros may be redefined as often as desired, the most recent definition applying at call time.

Single-pass restriction. Macros may be called only after they have been defined. This is to allow a single-pass macroprocessor to be written. Macros that are called before they are defined will therefore not be recognized as calls.

Again, myriad details have doubtless been omitted; they are left to the would-be implementer to resolve in any manner consistent with the principles set forth in Chapter 11.

Answers to Selected Exercises

Chapter 1

1. 0 and 1; bits.
2. The assembler translates the assembly language program into the corresponding machine language program.
3. Operation: describes the operation to be performed; operand: describes the locations of the data.
4. In the program counter (PC).
5. Yes.
6. a. *fact*.
   b. Register 6.
7. `mul3 a,a,b   ; b=a**2`
8. One.

Chapter 2

1. Virtual address extension. It means that most memory is located in secondary storage (disk) rather than in main memory.
2. 32; 2^{32}; a byte.
3. 8; $2^8 - 1 = 256 - 1$.
   16; $2^{16} - 1$.
   32; $2^{32} - 1$.
   64; $2^{64} - 1$.
4. R14.
5. R12 = AP—argument pointer; R13 = FP—frame pointer; R14 = SP—stack pointer; R15 = PC—program counter.
6. More addresses (called "virtual" addresses) can be referenced—2^{32} for the VAX rather than 2^{16} for the PDP-11.

Chapter 3

1. a. Binary sequences are harder to assimilate than hexadecimal sequences.
   b. It is easy to convert from hexadecimal to binary and vice versa.
   c. Storage sizes are multiples and divisors of 16.
2. a. 6F3D.
   b. B4F5.
   c. CA.
   d. 19.
3. a. 1000110001001110.
   b. 11110101.
   c. 01010110.
4. 00000000
   10000000.
5. 00000000
   11111111.
6. 1111111.
7. 11001011.
8. Do the steps of forming the two's complement in reverse:

Subtract: 11111110

−   1

11111101

Un-one's complement: 00000010 = 2

Therefore, the number is −2.

9. See Appendix A of *VAX-11 Architecture Handbook* [14].
10. The exponent is 10011100 = 156. Since 128 was added to it, the original exponent was 28. The fraction part is 0100001; thus, the original fraction was 10100001. The sign bit is 1, so the fraction is negative:

$$-.10100001_2 \times 2^{28} = -.62890625_{10} \times 2^{28} = -168820736.0$$

11. 61
    73
    63
    69
    69
12. No, since "b" is 62_{16} in ASCII and "B" is 42_{16} in ASCII.
13. `k: .byte 12`
14. `list: .blkb 6` or `list: .byte 0[6]`
15. Since 20 is the fourth number in the list and each number is stored in a word, the number 20 is in memory location 2006.

16. ;
```
; this program calculates the factorial of num
;
num:      .word   10
fact:     .word
;
begin:    .word
          movl    #1,fact         ; fact:=1
          movl    #1,r6           ; i:=1
loop:     mull2   r6,fact         ; fact:=fact*i
          aobleq  num,r6,loop     ; i:=i+1
          ret
          .end  begin
```
17. A binary point (what else?).

Chapter 4

1.
```
                  movw       #1,n
    loop:         incw       r6
                  decw       j
                  acbw       #100,#2,n,loop
```
2. ; this program calculates a**b for integers a and b
```
;
a:        .long   2
b:        .long   4
c:        .long
;
begin:    .word
          movl    #1,c        ; initialize c to 1
          movl    #1,r6       ; set loop counter to 1
loop:     mull2   a,c         ; c:=a*c
          aobleq  b,r6,loop ; check for finished loop
          ret
          .end  begin
```
4. The machine code for an addressing mode; a nibble.
5. Autodecrement and autoincrement.
6. 01011004.
7. Contents of the register contain the address of the operand, not the operand itself.
8. r_2 = 00002016; r_4 = 23016745.
9. ```movl r6,(r7)```

Chapter 5

We omit the answers to these questions to encourage you to code these problems for yourself. You can do it!

Chapter 6

1. a. Allows the programmer to write fewer lines of code.
   b. Makes the program more readable.
2. *.show me* causes the macro expansion to be listed in the assembly listing. If not present, the expansion is not listed.
3. The assembler expands each macro call by its corresponding definition.
4. *.macro* (at the beginning);
   .endm (at the end).
5–10. Give them a try. It's character building!

Chapter 7

1. LIFO list.
2. The stack grows toward lower addresses.
3. Yes—the stack holds longwords.
4. On the system stack.
5. Similar—both defined by the programmer once and used many times; different— macros expanded into their defining statements every time called.
6. (1) Transmit to the subroutine the address in the calling program to which it must return; (2) supply subroutine with the values for its parameters.
7. *calls, callg*
8. Linkage, argument transmission, return address are taken care of by the assembler.
9. (1) Pushing them onto stack; (2) placing them in registers; (3) putting their address into a register or onto the stack.
10.
```
result: .long
  args: .long   2,3,4
        .long   result
 start: .word
        pushal args
        jsb    calc
        addl2  #8,sp
          .

          .

          .
  calc: movl   4(sp),r1
        mull3  (r1)+,(r1)+,4(r1)
        addl3  (r1)+,(r1)+,@(r1)
        rsb
```

Bibliography

1. Alexander, W. G. and D. B. Wortman, "Static and Dynamic Characteristics in XPL Programs," *Computer Magazine,* Nov., 1975, Vol. 8 #11, pp. 41–46.
2. Bhanderkar, D., and S. Rothman, "The VAX-11: DEC's 32-bit version of the PDP-11," *Datamation,* February 1979, pp. 151–159.
3. Calingaert, Peter, *Assemblers, Compilers, and Program Translation,* (Potomac, Md.: Computer Science Press, 1979).
4. Elshoff, J. L., "A Numerical Profile of Commercial PL/I Programs," *Software Practice and Experience* 6, No. 4 (October–December 1976), 505–25.
5. Gear, C. William, *Introduction to Computers: Structured Programming and Applications, Module C, Computers and Systems* (SRA, 1978).
6. Gear, C. William, *Computer Organization and Programming* (New York: McGraw-Hill, 1980).
7. Gill, Arthur, *Machine and Assembly Language Programming of the PDP-11* (Englewood Cliffs, N.J.: Prentice-Hall, 1978).
8. Knuth, Donald E., "An Empirical Study of FORTRAN Programs," *Software Practice and Experience* 1, No. 2 (April–June 1971) pp. 105–133.
9. Levy, Henry M., and Richard E. Eckhouse, Jr., *Computer Programming and Architecture: The VAX-11* (Bedford, Mass.: Digital Press, 1980).
10. MacEwen, Glenn H., *Introduction to Computer Systems: Using the PDP-11 and Pascal,* (New York: McGraw-Hill, 1980).
11. Petersen, James I, *Computer Organization and Assembly Language Programming* (New York: Academic Press, 1978).

12. Robinson, S. K., and I. S. Torsun, "Empirical Analysis of FORTRAN Programs," *Computer Journal* 19 (1976), pp. 56–62.

13. Strecker, W. D., "Vax-11/780: A Virtual Address Extension to the PDP-11 Family," Proceedings of the NCC (Montvale, N.J.: AFIPS Press, 1978).

14. *VAX-11 Architecture Handbook* (Maynard, Mass.: Digital Equipment Corp., 1981).

15. *VAX-11 Command Language Users Guide* (Maynard, Mass.: Digital Equipment Corp., 1981).

16. *VAX-11/780 Hardware Handbook* (Maynard, Mass.: Digital Equipment Corp., 1982).

17. *VAX-11 Linker Reference Manual* (Maynard, Mass.: Digital Equipment Corp., 1981).

18. *VAX-11 MACRO Language Reference Manual* (Maynard, Mass.: Digital Equipment Corp., 1981).

19. *VAX-11 MACRO Language Users Guide* (Maynard, Mass.: Digital Equipment Corp., 1981).

20. *VAX-11 Primer* (Maynard, Mass.: Digital Equipment Corp., 1981).

21. *VAX-11 Software Handbook* (Maynard, Mass.: Digital Equipment Corp., 1982).

22. *VAX-11 Symbolic Debugger Reference Manual* (Maynard, Mass.: Digital Equipment Corp., 1981).

23. *VAX-11 Technical Summary* (Maynard, Mass.: Digital Equipment Corp., 1981).

24. Knuth, D. E., *The Art of Computer Programming,* Vol. III *Sorting and Searching* (Reading, Mass.: Addison-Wesley, 1973).

25. Donovan, John, *Systems Programming* (New York: McGraw-Hill, 1969).

26. *VAX-11 Record Management Services Reference Manual* (Maynard, Mass.: Digital Equipment Corp., 1981).

27. *VAX-11 Text Editing Reference Manual* (Maynard, Mass.: Digital Equipment Corp., 1981).

Index